W9-BKV-545

McGervey states that. . . .

- **The casino game that offers a player the best chance of coming out ahead (although the odds are *still* in favor of the house) is blackjack.**
- **The more money you bet on a single horse, the less favorable the odds will be. So it pays to bet in small increments at the track.**
- **When you play the stock market, switching from stock to stock, the "house edge" (the commissions you pay) is as tough to beat as it is at the horse races.**
- **A heavy smoker has over sixty times the risk of a nonsmoker of contracting lung cancer.**

PROBABILITIES IN EVERYDAY LIFE

John D. McGervey

IVY BOOKS • NEW YORK

Ivy Books
Published by Ballantine Books
Copyright © 1986 by John D. McGervey

All rights reserved under International and Pan-American Copyright Conventions. Published in the United States by Ballantine Books, a division of Random House, Inc., New York, and simultaneously in Canada by Random House of Canada Limited, Toronto.

No part of this book may be reproduced in any form without permission in writing from the publisher, except by a reviewer who wishes to quote brief passages in connection with a review written for broadcast or for inclusion in a magazine or newspaper. For information address Nelson-Hall Inc., Publishers, 111 North Canal Street, Chicago, Illinois 60606.

Library of Congress Catalog Card Number: 86-2406

ISBN 0-8041-0532-4

This edition published by arrangement with Nelson-Hall Publishers.

Manufactured in the United States of America

First Ballantine Books Edition: October 1989

CONTENTS

FOREWORD

by *Oswald Jacoby*

This is a fine book that is both entertaining and instructive. I am pleased to see that it is inspired, at least in part, by an early book of mine, *How to Figure the Odds*. But it is more than an updated version of that book; it gives unique insights into many new topics.

I have known John McGervey for thirty years, and I highly respect the accuracy of his analysis, which he has displayed at the bridge table and in bridge articles that he has written. He became a Life Master in bridge at the age of twenty-two, and he would be one of our really great players if he had not chosen to concentrate on a career in science. He is one of the best players, if not the very best player, among those who do not make playing bridge their major activity.

John has combined his experience in mathematics and in games to give helpful advice on practically anything that involves probabilities, which means practically anything at all. In the process, he has demolished a lot of myths that are bandied about by people who are fairly good at games but are not as good as they could be because they haven't mastered the science of probability.

John's first book was a textbook on modern physics and quantum theory. That book became well known for its clear presentation of a difficult subject, and it is now in a second edition. It succeeded because it presented physics in a lively way, and John has now done the same thing for probability.

PREFACE

My study of physics and mathematics, as well as my interest in games, has naturally led to a fascination with probability. Unfortunately, it is sometimes painful to see how the subject has been abused in books and in the media—for example, the countless misconceptions, the misuse of statistics, the prevalence of unsound gambling systems, and the misunderstanding of hazards and insurance.

College students with an aptitude for mathematics are not immune to these problems, and many of them never get a taste of down-to-earth applications of probability. For that reason, when Case Western Reserve University solicited the faculty for ideas for new and innovative short courses, I was happy to offer a course in "gambling," in the broadest sense of the word. The course was well received, and it inspired me to write this book, which I hope will save you some money as well as entertain you.

Most of the book can be read easily by anyone who is not afraid to see a few numbers and an occasional algebraic equation. The treatment of statistical distributions [chapter 3] is as simplified as one can make it without pulling results out of thin air. Readers who find it heavy going, however, can just accept the results and move on. The results are quite useful later in the book.

I have tried as far as possible to encourage the reader not to accept anybody's opinion [not even mine] on faith. Readers have ways of checking things out for themselves, and the book suggests a number of tests that can be made.

I couldn't have covered such a variety of topics without help, and I am grateful to the organizations listed in the footnotes throughout the text. In addition, I want to thank the people at the Allen Memorial Medical Library at Case Western Reserve University, the Ohio Motorists Association, Alcoholics Anonymous, the Gambler's Book Club, and the National Institute on Drug Abuse for their help in finding information.

Special thanks are due to my daughter, Anne, who helped to program our computer, and to the great gambling expert, the late Oswald Jacoby, who read almost all of the manuscript before his death in 1984 and provided useful suggestions and encouragement. Friends and colleagues who also read sections, provided suggestions, or both, included Dr. Ben Green, Professor Stefan Machlup, Dennis McGarry, Lawrence J. Rock, Alfred P. Sheinwold, and Dr. Virginia F. Walters. Of course responsibility for any remaining mistakes is solely mine.

CHAPTER 1

Principles and Propositions

The science of probability originated with a betting proposition, so let us begin by analyzing a few simple propositions as we develop the general principles. We will find that the same basic principles can be applied over and over again to work out all the probabilities that you will ever want to know.

Definitions

The first step is to define what we mean by probability. Suppose we bet that a certain event will occur (for example, it will rain tomorrow). Winning your bet is called a favorable result; all other results (for example, fair and warmer) are called unfavorable results. Let us further suppose that you could repeat that bet thousands of times under apparently identical conditions (for example, the weather map looks the same). Then the probability that you will win your bet on any specific occasion is given by the ratio

$$\text{Probability} = \frac{\text{Number of favorable results}}{\text{Total number of bets}}$$

We see from this definition of probability that any probability must be a number between zero and one, inclusive. An impossible result has a probability of zero; a sure thing has a probability of one.

We don't actually have to bet in order to define probability. We could make a test, or "trial," of various possible outcomes simply by observing what happens. Then we have

1

$$\text{Probability of favorable result} = \frac{\text{Number of favorable results}}{\text{Total number of trials}}$$

Furthermore, we don't even have to go through with the trials in order to decide upon a value for the probability in many cases. For example, we don't toss a coin a million times to find the probability that it will come up "heads" when it is tossed. If we can't find any reason for the coin to come up heads rather than tails (or vice versa), we just assume that both results will occur an equal number of times in a large number of trials.[1] In that case, the probability of heads is 1/2, and so is the probability of tails. [We have all done enough trials of coin tossing to rule out any other result as a significant possibility.]

Similarly, a die has six faces, numbered one through six. We assume that in a large[2] number of trials, a given face will come up just about as often as any other face, or on 1/6 of the total number of throws of the dice. So we deduce that the probability of rolling any given number is 1/6.

This leads us to an alternative definition, the so-called a priori definition of probability, which we state in two steps:

1. If we can find no reason why one result should occur more often than another result, then we can say that both results are equally probable.[3]

2. If the only possible results of a trial are all equally probable, then the probability that any one of these results will occur on a given trial is:

$$\text{Probability} = \frac{1}{\text{Number of possible results}}$$

Thus, for a roll of one die, we say that each of the six numbers is equally probable, and the probability of getting, say, a "two" is 1/6. This seems too simple to bother using so many words. But when we consider the probabilities of various totals on the roll of two dice, we see that we must be careful.

There are eleven possibilities [two through twelve], but

they are not equally probable because we can find a reason why one total might appear more often than another. Imagine that we roll the dice one at a time. After we roll a six on the first die, then the probability of a total of twelve is 1/6 (we just need another six on the second die), and the probability of a total of seven is also 1/6 (we need a one on the second die). But if we roll anything except a six on the first die, a total of twelve is impossible, and a total of seven still has a probability of 1/6. So seven has to be more probable than twelve initially.

Combined Probability

Dice throwing has shown us a situation in which we want to find the probability that two independent events—the appearance of a given number on each of two dice—will both occur. When we say that the events are independent, we mean that the occurrence of one event does not affect the probability that the other event will occur. The second die does not observe what the first die has done in order to decide what it will do. It is easy to show that, in such a case, the probability that both events will occur is the product of two separate probabilities:

$$\text{Probability of A } and \text{ B} =$$
$$\text{Probability of A} \times \text{Probability of B}$$

If the events are not independent, which means that the probability of B depends on whether or not A occurs, the rule is unchanged except that we must use the probability of B that applies when we know that A has occurred. We shall see an example of this in the "birthday proposition" discussed below.

To show how and why this rule works, let us find the probability of rolling two dice to produce a specific number on each die—say a "one" on each of the two dice. The probability of a one on the first die is 1/6, and the probability of a one on the second die is also 1/6. Therefore the probability of a one on both dice is 1/6 × 1/6, or 1/36. We get the same answer from the original definition of probability if we are patient enough to roll the dice often enough. For example, on 36,000 rolls, we will get a one on the first [honest] die about 6,000 times. On these 6,000 rolls, we will get a one on the second [honest] die 1,000 times. So the probability of getting both ones is 1,000/36,000, or 1/36.

Another simple rule concerns the probability that one or another of two or more mutually exclusive events will occur. [If two events are mutually exclusive, both cannot occur on the same trial.] The rule is

> Probability of A *or* B =
> Probability of A + Probability of B

For example, the probability of rolling a total of three on two dice is the probability that one or the other of two events will occur: A: "one" followed by "two"; B: "two" followed by "one." These are clearly mutually exclusive, and therefore the combined probability is the sum of the probability of A and the probability of B, 1/36 + 1/36, or 1/18.

Dice Probabilities and "Odds"

We can find the probability of any other total, or "point," on two dice just by adding the probabilities (of 1/36) for each way that the point can come up. The results are shown in table 1-1.

Later we'll apply these probabilities to some popular games. For now, let's look at some simple propositions, or "side bets," that could tempt you when dice are being thrown. For example, a stranger might bet you that a seven will appear before a six. To analyze this bet, we ignore the twenty-five combinations that give neither six nor seven. There are eleven ways that the bet can be decided; six ways win for the stranger—a seven comes up—and only five ways win for you. If you repeatedly accept bets like this, you will become very popular with people who don't want to work for a living.

But perhaps the stranger does not really want to cheat you;

Table 1-1. Points with Two Dice

Point	Ways to roll point	Number of ways	Probability
2	1–1	1	1/36
3	1–2, 2–1	2	1/18
4	1–3, 2–2, 3–1	3	1/12
5	1–4, 2–3, 3–2, 4–1	4	1/9
6	1–5, 2–4, 3–3, 4–2, 5–1	5	5/36
7	1–6, 2–5, 3–4, 4–3, 5–2, 6–1	6	1/6
8	2–6, 3–5, 4–4, 5–3, 6–2	5	5/36
9	3–6, 4–5, 5–4, 6–3	4	1/9
10	4–6, 5–5, 6–4	3	1/12
11	5–6, 6–5	2	1/18
12	6–6	1	1/36

he may just like to gamble. In that case, he will offer you "odds" of 6 to 5; that is, he will bet \$6 against your \$5. Then, on eleven "average" trials, he will win six bets of \$5 each, you will win five bets of \$6 each, and it will be a fair bet. In general, a "fair bet" is one in which the amount of money put up by each bettor is proportional to the bettor's probability of winning the bet, or to the "true odds" on the bet.

The true odds are the ratio of the probabilities on the two sides of a bet. If event A is only one of several possible events, then

$$\text{Odds against A} = \frac{\text{Probability that A does not occur}}{\text{Probability that A does occur}}$$

For example, if you bet on an event A whose probability of occurrence is 1/10, the probability that A does not occur is 9/10, and the odds against A are 9 to 1. In the bet discussed above (six vs. seven on two dice), the probability of six is 5/11 (not 5/36). This is because a "trial" can only be a roll that results in a "six" or a "seven," and "six" constitutes five of the eleven possible results of such a trial.

You will sometimes read that the odds "of" something happening are "a thousand to one." I don't know what that means. From the context, you can usually guess that the odds *against* that occurrence are 1,000 to 1.

When the odds against something are less than 1 to 1, they might be quoted as, say, 2 to 3. In such a case, we say that this is "odds on" to occur, and a person betting on the event must "give odds."

Dice Propositions

Many people know the odds against any particular point in a dice game, but they can still be fooled by propositions involving combined probability. One such proposition led to the development of the science of probability.

The mathematician Blaise Pascal had a friend, the Chevalier de Mere, who was making money by betting that he could get at least one "six" on four rolls of one die. The Chevalier knew from experience that this bet was profitable for him, but eventually his victims also learned from experience, and his business slumped.

To keep his action going, he began to bet that he could get a twelve on twenty-four rolls of two dice. This seemed logical; although he had only 1/6 as great a chance on each roll [1/36 instead of 1/6], he had six times as many rolls. But before long he realized that he was losing money on these bets, and he asked Pascal to analyze the proposition.

Pascal's calculation was elegant and simple. He worked the problem "backwards," by considering the probability that a twelve is *not* rolled. For one roll, this probability is 35/36. For two rolls, he worked out our first rule, that is, the probability that events A and B *both* occur is equal to the probability of A times the probability of B. If event A is "non-twelve on first roll," and event B is "non-twelve on second roll," each event has a probability of 35/36. The probability of non-twelve on two rolls must then be $(35/36)^2$, and by extending the argument we find that the probability of non-twelve on twenty-four rolls must be $(35/36)^{24}$, or about 51%. So the Chevalier figured to lose 51% of his bets.

A modern day dice proposition that still claims victims was described by Oswald Jacoby as follows:

Early in the game [a] major bet [a] colonel even money that the shooter would roll an eight before he rolled a seven. The colonel concealed his pleasure at getting even money when he should be laying 6 to 5. A few minutes later the major bet that the shooter would roll a six before he rolled a seven. The colonel took that bet also. After losing a few bets of this kind, the major said, "This one-roll stuff is too much like sudden death. I'll bet you on eight and six before he gets *two* sevens."

The colonel didn't even feel the hook when he took this bet. He must have thought the major was very lucky to win so many of these bets during the course of the evening, but if he ever sees this he will know that he was given a build-up appropriate to his rank.[4]

The "hook" is that the bet didn't specify which point the shooter had to get first; the major won if the shooter got a six followed by an eight or an eight followed by a six. This gave the major ten ways [instead of five] to get his first point, while the colonel still had the same six ways for the roll of a seven.

Let's say that the major wins a "trial" by getting the number he needs, and the colonel wins a trial by getting a seven. Winning two trials out of three wins the bet. Then the total probability of a win for the major can be broken into two parts: First, he can win the first trial and then win one of the next two. His chance of winning the first trial is $10/16$. After winning that, his chance of losing the next two is $(6/11)^2$, so the chance that he does *not* lose the next two must be $1 - (6/11)^2$. Multiplying this by $10/16$ gives us the probability for the first part.

Second, he can lose the first trial and then win the next two. You can work out for yourself that this second probability is $(6/16) \times (10/16) \times (5/11)$. Adding this to the first probability gives the major a total probability of $4,225/7,744$, or about 54.6%; the odds against the colonel are $4,225$ to $3,519$, or about 6 to 5.

Mathematical Expectation

A very useful definition is that of the expectation on a bet. Assume that you make a large number of identical bets on identical situations. Then

$$\text{Expectation} = \frac{\text{Total money returned to you}}{\text{Total number of bets}}$$

This is the same as the product of the return on each bet and the probability of winning that bet. For example, if the major and the colonel were betting $10 each time, the winner would receive $20 and the major's expectation would be 4,225/7,744 times $20, or $10.91. Each time the colonel made one of these bets, he would be giving the major $.91.

The ratio of the average loss [$.91 in this case] to the amount bet [$10 in this case] would be called the "house percentage" in a casino. In Jacoby's story, the major was very ably playing the role of the house, with a house percentage of 9.1%. In later chapters we'll see how to figure house percentages in a real "house," as well as in such diverse activities as buying stocks and investing in collectibles.

The Birthday Proposition

At a crowded party where most of the people are strangers to each other, a "friend" offers to bet you $10 that at least two of the people in the room have the same birthday. Being a bit suspicious, you say, "Let's bet on the people in the next room." Seeing 29 people in that room, he agrees. What would you guess is your probability of winning, assuming that your friend has no advance information on anyone's birthday?

We assume that one birthday is just as likely as any other,[5] so the probability that the second birthday is different from the first is 364/365 [forget leap year]. If it is, then the chance that the third birthday falls on one of the remaining 363 days is 363/365, and the combined probability that all three are different is [364/365] × [363/365]. By extending this reasoning, we find that the probability that all twenty-nine people have different birthdays is a number with twenty-eight factors: [364/365] × [363/365] × [362/365] × . . . × [337/365]. The final result is a probability of .319, or only 31.9%, that you will win.

How did your friend know that he had such huge odds—better than 2 to 1—going for him? He probably didn't know the exact odds, but he did know that with only twenty-three people he had a better than even chance and that the extra six people were just gravy.

If you have a really large group of people, you might hear a reverse twist on the birthday proposition. Somebody could offer to bet that nobody in a group of, say, 200 people has the same birthday as yours. It could be tempting to accept this bet because you might think that each person gives you a chance of 1/365, and that 200 people would give you a chance of 200/365—more than 50%. But you can add such probabilities only if the events are mutually exclusive, and these are not. Having one person match your birthday does not rule out the possibility that another person can also match your birthday.

The correct way to find this probability is to use the method that Pascal applied to the Chevalier's problem. The probability that any given person does not match your birthday is 364/365, and therefore the probability that 200 people do not match it is $[364/365]^{200}$. This works out to be .578, leaving you a probability of only .422 of finding a match.

To have a 50% chance on this proposition, you need 253 people. Why so many? Because many of the people match each other. Among 253 people, you will find, on the average, only 183 different birthdays. You have about a 50% chance that your birthday is one of these 183 instead of the other 182. If you had the time to try this on a hundred groups, of 253 people each, you would get the following [approximate] distribution:

- 50 groups give no match
- 35 groups give one match
- 12 groups give two matches
- 3 groups give three matches

The total number of matches is about 68, which is what you should expect from 25,300 people. The derivation of these numbers will be explained when we discuss statistical distributions in chapter 2.

Exercises

Here are some more propositions of the type discussed above. You may want to try deciding for yourself whether you should take the bet that is offered. Solutions are given below.

1. Opponent offers to bet even money that, on a roll of three dice, all three numbers will be different.

2. Opponent wants to bet even money that, on two dice, a five and a nine will appear (in either order) before two sevens.

3. Opponent offers to bet $6 to your $5 that he will get a pair in six cards dealt from a regular deck of fifty-two cards.

4. Opponent offers to bet $6 to your $5 that, if you deal three cards from this deck, two of them will be in the same suit (any suit).

5. There are three cards in a hat. One is red on both sides, one is blue on both sides, and one is red on one side and blue on the other side. You pull out a card just far enough so you and your opponent can see that it is red on one side. Now he offers to bet $6 to your $5 that it is also red on the other side.

6. A jar contains four white balls and one red ball. A second jar contains four red balls and one white ball. You reach into one of the two jars (neither you nor your opponent knows which jar) and you pull out a red ball. Now he offers to bet $6 to your $5 that the next ball you pull from that same jar will be red.

7. On the street, your friend offers to bet on auto license plates that contain at least two numerals. He will bet that the next twenty plates will include two that match in the last two digits.

Solutions

1. Don't bet. The probability that all three are different is [5/6] × [4/6], or 5/9, so the odds are 5 to 4 against you.

2. Take the bet. His probability of winning the first trial and then winning one of the next two is [8/14] × [1 − [6/10]²], which equals .3657. His probability of losing the first trial and winning the next two is [6/14] × [8/14] × [4/10], which equals .0980. His total chance of winning is 46.4%.

3. Don't bet. The probability that all six are of different rank is [48/51] × [44/50] × [40/49] × [36/48] × [32/47]. This comes to about 7/23, so the odds against you are 16 to 7. Any poker player knows that the probability of getting a pair in five cards is less than 50%, but the last factor of 32/47 makes a big difference.

4. Don't bet. The probability that all three are in different suits is [39/51] × [26/50], which equals 169/425, so the odds against you are 256 to 169, or about 3 to 2.

5. Don't bet. It is logical to assume that all six sides of the cards are equally likely to be seen. There are three red sides, and two of them are on the double-red card. Therefore the probability is 2/3 that you are seeing that card, and the odds are 2 to 1 against you if you bet.

6. Don't bet. Four of the five red balls are in the second jar; given that you drew a red ball, the probability is 4/5 that you drew it from that jar. The probability of getting a second red ball from the jar is 3/4, so the overall probability of getting a second red ball is [4/5] × [3/4], or 3/5. [Of course if you did draw the lone red ball from the first jar, the probability of getting another red ball is nil.]

7. Don't bet. This is the birthday proposition in disguise with 100 possibilities instead of 365. The chance that there is no match is .99 × .98 × . . . . 81, which works out to a mere 13%. Your "friend" would have a roughly even chance after only twelve plates! In general, when there are n equally likely possibilities, there is an even chance of a match when the number of samples is approximately $\sqrt{1.4n}$. With n equal to 100, $\sqrt{1.4n} = \sqrt{140} \approx 12$. For the original birthday proposition, with n equal to 365, $\sqrt{1.4n} = \sqrt{511} \approx 23$. If you are interested in the derivation of this number, see the discussion of the number e, the base of natural logarithms, in chapter 2.

CHAPTER 2

Statistics

Statistics are a natural companion to probability. We saw that the basic definition of probability is based upon the accumulation of statistics, and we can predict future statistics (for example, automobile deaths on holiday weekends) with a reliability that is limited by the laws of probability. In this chapter we explore the connection between probability and statistics and give guidelines for determining when a statistic is significant.

Statistical Distributions

If we kept track of the results of a thousand rolls of two dice, we could construct a statistical distribution that would follow the probabilities in table 1-1, with each number approximately a thousand times larger. But each number would not be exactly a thousand times the corresponding probability. The science of statistics tells us how much deviation to expect.

Knowledge of the expected deviation can help us avoid the pitfall of assuming that every little fluctuation in a statistic must have an "explanation." If the number of traffic deaths in our city this year is up 20% from last year's results, and therefore we consider firing the police chief, we should first determine the significance of that 20%. A rise from 200 to 240 might be statistically significant, but a rise from 10 to 12 is not, even though each is a 20% increase.

We must be sure that we understand the meaning of the word *significant* in this context. The death of a single human

13

being is significant. But statistical significance is a technical term that tells us whether some systematic reason must be behind a given result. Some policymakers confuse the ordinary meaning with the technical meaning by asserting that a course of action is justified if it does not result in a statistically significant number of deaths. For example, an administrator in the environmental protection agency approved the release of pollutants estimated to kill 1 person in 10,000. The rationale was that no study could ever reveal a statistically significant increase in the death rate.[1]

To see how we determine the significance of a statistic, let's first look at the numbers that result from coin tossing or dice throwing, activities for which we know what to expect.

Binomial Distribution

In dice throwing or coin tossing you make many "trials," and (presumably) each trial gives exactly the same probability of success as any other trial. Under these conditions, the set of probabilities of 0, 1, 2, etc., successes on a given number of trials is called a binomial distribution.

For example, go back to the Chevalier's original proposition [chapter 1] to get at least one six in four rolls of a single die. We solved this proposition by finding the probability of getting no sixes, $(5/6)^4$, or 625/1,296. To find the probability distribution, we also need the probabilities of one, two, three, or four sixes.

One Six. The probability of getting a six on the first roll, and no six on the other rolls, is $(1/6) \times (5/6)^3$, or 125/1,296. The total probability of getting exactly one six includes the probability that the six will come on the second, third, or fourth roll as well. Each of these is also 125/1,296, making a total probability of 500/1,296.

Two sixes. The probability of getting a six on the first roll and on the second roll, but not on the third or fourth rolls, must be $(1/6)^2 \times (5/6)^2$, or 25/1,296. We could also get two sixes by getting a six on the first and third, first and fourth, second and third, second and fourth, or third and fourth rolls, giving us a total of six different ways. So the total probability of two sixes is $6 \times 25/1{,}296$, or $150/1{,}296$.

Three or four sixes. In a similar way, we can see that the probability of getting three sixes is $4 \times [1/6]^3 \times [5/6]$, or $20/1{,}296$, and for four sixes it is $[1/6]^4$, or $1/1{,}296$. Thus the overall distribution is:

Number of Sixes:	Probability:
0	625/1,296
1	500/1,296
2	150/1,296
3	20/1,296
4	1/1,296

These probabilities add up to 1, as they must, because no other result is possible.

Working out a probability distribution by identifying all of the possibilities, as we have done here, can be tedious, especially when more trials are involved. It is easier to use a general formula for the probability of s successes in terms of n, the number of trials, and p, the probability of success on each trial. This probability is the product of two factors:

$p^s(1 - p)^{n-s}$ The probability of getting the s successes on a particular set of s trials.

$\dfrac{n!}{(n - s)!s!}$ The number of possible sets of s trials out of a total of n trials. This number is the number of combinations of s objects selected from n objects, often denoted by the symbol $C[n, s]$.

Putting these together, we find that the probability of s successes in n trials, with probability p of success in each trial, called the *binomial probability*, is

$$P_b[n, s] = C[n, s]p^s(1 - p)^{n-s} \qquad [2 - 1]$$

We shall encounter many applications of the factor $C[n, s]$. For example, $C[13, 5]$ is the number of 5-card combina-

Table 2-1. Values of C[n, s]

s =	0	1	2	3	4	5	6	7	8	9	10	11	12	2^n
n = 0	1													1
1	1	1												2
2	1	2	1											4
3	1	3	3	1										8
4	1	4	6	4	1									16
5	1	5	10	10	5	1								32
6	1	6	15	20	15	6	1							64
7	1	7	21	35	35	21	7	1						128
8	1	8	28	56	70	56	28	8	1					256
9	1	9	36	84	126	126	84	36	9	1				512
10	1	10	45	120	210	252	210	120	45	10	1			1,024
11	1	11	55	165	330	462	462	330	165	55	11	1		2,048
12	1	12	66	220	495	792	924	792	495	220	66	12	1	4,096

tions that can be selected from a thirteen-card suit [for example, the number of heart flushes that are possible in poker].

Pascal Triangle

The values of C[n, s] can be displayed in a pattern called the Pascal triangle, shown in Table 2-1 for n up to 12.

As you can see, each number in this triangle is equal to the sum of two numbers in the row above it—the number directly above and the number above and to the left. This makes the total for each row twice the total for the row above it, and the total for the nth row equal to 2^n, as shown in the right-hand column. [This total has to be 2^n to make the sum of the probabilities equal to 1.]

The Pascal triangle makes it easy to compute cases with $p = 1/2$; you just pick out C[n, s] and divide it by 2^n. For example, if the Toledo Mud Hens have a 50% probability of winning each game of a six-game series, the probability that the Mud Hens will win exactly three games is C[6, 3]/2^6, or 20/64. [It may surprise you that a six-game series between evenly matched teams will usually split unevenly.]

Before going further with the binomial distribution, let's look at other related distributions.

Poisson Distribution

We have seen that the binomial distribution is determined by the number of trials (n) and the probability of success on each trial (p). In many everyday situations, neither n nor p is known, but we do know the product of n and p, which we call m, the mean number of successes.

For many of these situations n is very large and p is close to zero. For example, a large number of pedestrians cross streets every day, and the probability that a given pedestrian will be hit by a car on any given occasion is very small. In this case, the numbers of pedestrians who are hit each week follow the Poisson distribution, which is the limiting case of a binomial distribution as n approaches infinity and p approaches zero, while the product np, the mean number of "successes," remains constant. We'll use the symbol $P_P[m, s]$ to represent the Poisson probability for s successes when the mean is m.

To find the formula for $P_P[m, s]$, we'll start with the case $m = 1$. The mean m will be 1 if n and p have any of the sets of values listed below; for each set, the probability of zero successes is shown as $P[1,0]$ [equal to $(1 - p)^n$, or $(1 - 1/n)^n$]:

n	p	P(1, 0)		
10	.1	$.9^{10}$	=	.34867844 . . .
100	.01	$.99^{100}$	=	.36603234 . . .
1,000	.001	$.999^{1000}$	=	.36769542 . . .
10,000	.0001	$.9999^{10000}$	=	.36786105 . . .

P without a subscript is the binomial probability expressed in terms of m and s rather than n and s.

As n gets larger and larger and p approaches zero, $P[1, 0]$ approaches a limiting value of "approximately" .36787944, which is $P_P[1, 0]$. The precise limit can be calculated to any desired degree of accuracy, and it is a well-known number, e^{-1}, where e is the base of natural logarithms ["approximately" 2.718281828459045].

If you know a little calculus, you will recognize that this

result follows directly from the definition of e: e is the limit of $[1 + 1/x]^x$ as x goes to infinity, and therefore e^{-1} is the limit of $[1 + 1/x]^{-x}$, which becomes $[1 - 1/n]^n$ with the substitution $x = -n$.

If the probability of zero successes is e^{-1} when the mean m is 1, what is the probability of zero successes for other values of m? It is easy to show that, in general, this probability is e^{-m}. We construct a new list like the one above, but with np equal to m:

n	p	P(m, 0)
10m	.1	$.9^{10m}$
100m	.01	$.99^{100m}$
1,000m	.001	$.999^{1,000m}$

When comparing $P[m, 0]$ with $P[1, 0]$, we see that a factor of m appears in the exponent. Therefore the exponent in the limit must also contain this factor, and since $P_p[1, 0]$ equals e^{-1}, $P_p[m, 0]$ must equal e^{-m}.

To find the probability of any other number of successes, we can go back to the binomial formula 2-1. By canceling terms in $C[n, s]$, we can write the binomial formula as

$$P_b[n, s] = \frac{n[n - 1] \times \ldots \times [n - s + 1]}{s!} \, p^s (1 - p)^{n-s}$$

But since n is so large, we can approximate the factors $n - 1$, $n - 2$, etc., each as n, so the result becomes

$$P_b[n, s] = n^s p^s (1 - p)^n / s!$$

The factor $[1 - p]^n$ again becomes e^{-m}, and we find that the Poisson probability for s successes, when the mean number of successes is m, is

$$P_p[m, s] = m^s e^{-m} / s!$$

For example, if the number of persons kicked by mules in a certain county in Arkansas is three per year, then the probability that nobody will be kicked in a given year is e^{-3}, the probability that exactly one person will be kicked is $3e^{-3}$, that two will be kicked is $3^2e^{-3}/2$, etc.

Figure 2-1 shows all of the probabilities for $m = 3$, and it shows two other probability distributions for which m is also 3, a binomial distribution with $n = 6$ and $p = 1/2$ and a binomial distribution with $n = 18$ and $p = 1/6$. The latter would give the probabilities for various numbers of ones on eighteen rolls of a single die.

For very improbable events we don't have to consider any number of successes except zero or one. For example, suppose there are a million tickets sold each year on the Irish Sweepstakes. If you bought one ticket every year, your mean number of successes in twenty years would be $20/1,000,000$, or 0.00002. Your probability of zero successes would be e^{-m}, which is approximately $.99998$, and your probability of one success would be me^{-m}, approximately equal to m, or $.00002$. [The sum of these two probabilities is 1, which would mean that *two* successes are impossible. That is not strictly true. According to Poisson statistics, your chance of two successes is about $.0000000002$.] So in this case it is OK just to add your probabilities each year. A probability of one in a million each year for twenty years gives you a probability of twenty in a million.

Normal Distribution

Binomial and Poisson distributions can be computed exactly for any value of m. We have, for example, computed the distribution of probabilities of various numbers of deaths resulting from the exposure of one million people to the above-mentioned pollutant [which was estimated to kill one person in 10,000]. The mean in this case is 100, and the results are shown in Figure 2-2. Each bar shows the Poisson probability of the corresponding number of ''successes''— that is, deaths. We see the probability that exactly 100 would die is about 4% and the probability that exactly 90 would die is about 2.5%. We also see that the probabilities roughly follow the ''bell-shaped'' solid line shown in figure 2-2.

Figure 2-1. Probability P_r of r occurrences of an event in n trials if probability of occurrence is p on each trial. (a) Binomial distribution, $n = 6$, $p = 1/2$. (b) Binomial distribution, $n = 18$, $p = 1/6$. (c) Poisson distribution, limiting case of binomial distribution, with $n \to \infty$, $p \to 0$, but $np = 3$ as in (a) and (b).

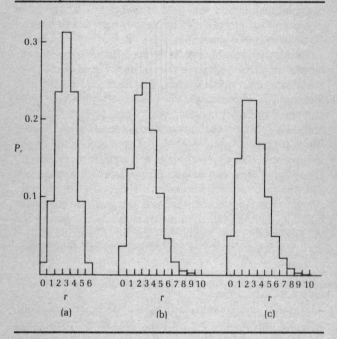

SOURCE: John D. McGervey, *Introduction to Modern Physics*, 2d ed. (New York: Academic Press, 1983).

We could plot the binomial distribution for $p = 1/2$ and $m = 100$ in the same way. The bars would again follow a "bell-shaped" curve, but the actual probabilities are different for this case. For 100 "successes" the probability is 5.6% instead of 4%, and for $s = 90$ it is only 2% instead of 2.5%. So the "bell" that fits this distribution is taller and narrower than the one in figure 2-2.

Figure 2-2. Poisson distribution for $m = 100$. Solid line shows the normal distribution which most closely fits this Poisson distribution, with $\sigma = 10$.

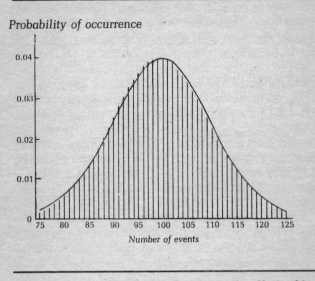

Probability of occurrence

Number of events

SOURCE: John D. McGervey, *Introduction to Modern Physics*, 2d ed. (New York: Academic Press, 1983).

However, both bell-shaped curves share the same mathematical properties and are called "Gaussian" curves. A probability distribution that follows a Gaussian curve is called a *normal* distribution. Neither the Poisson distribution nor the binomial distribution is exactly "normal" for any finite value of m, but they approach the normal distribution more closely as m increases. When m equals 100, they are close enough to "normal" for most practical purposes.

The difference between these two distributions is expressed mathematically by the standard deviation (symbol σ). "Deviation" here is the difference between the value of s and the mean m. To find the standard deviation, we take the average (the arithmetic mean) of the squares of all the deviations for the entire distribution, and then we take the square root of the result. Thus σ is the "root-mean-squared" [rms] deviation.

Fortunately, for these probability distributions we don't have to go to the trouble of squaring all the deviations and finding the average. There is a general result that, for any binomial distribution, σ is approximately equal to $\sqrt{m(1-p)}$. For the Poisson distribution this reduces to $\sqrt{m}$, because $p = 0$.

The standard deviation is useful because it completely describes the normal distribution for a given m. It permits you to find the probability of any given result or group of results, simply by referring to a table such as table 2-2. For example, the table gives a probability of 15.87% that s exceeds m by more than one standard deviation. There is also a probability of 15.87% that s is *less* than m by one standard deviation or more. So the probability that s is within one standard deviation of m is about 68% [100% − 2 × 15.87%].

To apply the normal distribution to a specific case, you have to remember that it is a smooth curve that is exactly applicable only when the number of trials is infinite. To find the probabilities when n is finite, the prescription is as follows:

1. Chop up the normal curve into segments of length one so that there is one segment for each value of s. For example, the probability for $s = 101$ is given by the segment between 100.5 and 101.5.

2. Find the deviation from the mean at each end of the segment; with $m = 100$ and $s = 101$, the deviations would be 0.5 and 1.5.

3. Express each deviation as a multiple of the standard deviation. For $\sigma = 10$, the above deviations are .05σ and .15σ.

4. Look up the "Probability of a greater deviation" in table 2-2; you will find .4801 for .05σ, and .4404 for .15σ.

5. Take the difference between the two probabilities given in the table; this is your answer, .0397 in this case, for $s = 101$.

Table 2-2. Normal Distribution

Deviation/σ	Probability of a greater deviation	Deviation/σ	Probability of a greater deviation
0	.5000	1.00	.1587
.05	.4801	1.25	.1056
.10	.4602	1.50	.06681
.15	.4404	1.75	.04006
.20	.4207	2.00	.02275
.25	.4013	2.25	.01222
.30	.3821	2.50	.00621
.35	.3632	2.75	.00298
.40	.3446	3.00	.00135
.45	.3264	3.25	.00058
.50	.3085	3.50	.00023
.55	.2912	3.75	.000088
.60	.2742	4.00	.000032
.65	.2578	4.50	.0000034
.70	.2420	5.00	3×10^{-7}
.75	.2266	6.00	1×10^{-9}
.80	.2119		
.85	.1977		
.90	.1841		
.95	.1711		

That looks like a lot of work but it is really quite simple, and it can be very accurate when m is large. For the example shown here, the exact result obtained from the Poisson formula is .0395 instead of .0397. [You can see in figure 2-2 that the bar representing the Poisson probability is just a trifle too short to reach the "normal" curve at $s = 10$.] You can also judge the accuracy of results for other values of s from that figure.]

This prescription can also be used to find the probability of a range of values of s. Let's look at a concrete example. Willie Wacker has a lifetime batting average of .300. Last year, however, he batted 525 times and got only 147 hits, for an average of .280. Is Willie, who is thirty years old, over the hill, or was he just unlucky last year? To try to answer this, we first must realize that the probability of batting *exactly* .280 is very small; we want the probability of batting .280 or worse to evaluate Willie's luck.

The probability of 147 or fewer hits is found by "chopping" the normal curve at 147.5, which is 10 below Willie's lifetime mean of 157.5 [.3 of 525]. The standard deviation is $\sqrt{.7 \times 157.5} = \sqrt{110.5} = 10.5$, and therefore we want the probability of a result that is 10/10.5 standard deviations below the mean. Table 2-2 shows that this is about 17 percent.

To decide whether Willie is over the hill, we really need more information about his physical condition. Experience with other players, however, suggests that it is rather unusual to go downhill at thirty, so it seems more likely that Willie just had bad luck. Of course that won't prevent George, the team's owner, from crying that Willie isn't earning his big salary. Conversely, if Willie had batted .320, it seems that Lady Luck would deserve the credit, but dozens of reporters would have interviewed him to ask the reason for his sudden "improvement."

Generally we consider a deviation of three or more standard deviations from the mean to be sufficiently rare [only 0.3% probable] that it can be called "statistically significant." This means that, when we see such a deviation, we should suspect that the distribution is not what we thought it was. Thus if Willie had batted .240, we would have good reason to believe that something was wrong with him, and we would look for the cause if it were not otherwise obvious. [Maybe he needs new eyeglasses.]

Exercises

Here are a few simple manipulations to reinforce what we have discussed here. Solutions follow.

1. How many different three-digit combinations are there, using each of the digits 0 through 9 only once? [012, 021, 102, 120, 201, and 210 collectively count as a single combination.]

2. Find the probability of rolling three or more sevens on twenty rolls of two dice.

3. If the mean number of traffic deaths on a weekend is 400, find the probability that there will be fewer than 350 deaths on an otherwise normal weekend. Also find the probability that there will be exactly 410 deaths.

4. The probability of getting exactly five heads on ten flips of an honest coin is 252/1,024 [about 25%; see table 2-1]. Use the normal distribution [table 2-2] to show that the probability of exactly fifty heads on 100 flips of a coin is only 7.96%. Things don't "even out" in the long run, do they?

5. Use the Poisson probability to find the general formula for the "birthday proposition" [chapter 1]. That is, if there are N equally likely birthdates in a year and n people are chosen at random, what value of n is needed to make the probability of having a match be at least 1/2? [Assume that $n \ll N$.]

Solutions

1. This is [C10,3], which equals $10 \times 9 \times 8/3!$, or 120.

2. 33.0%.

3. This number follows a Poisson distribution with $m = 400$, which can be approximated well by a normal distribution with $\sigma = 20$. The probability of a deviation of more than 2.5 in one direction is given by table 2-2 as .00621. ["Chopping" the curve at 350 instead of 349.5 makes little difference in this result.]

5. The probability of no match is e^{-m}, where m is the mean number of matches expected when you choose n persons. To make this probability equal to 1/2, m must equal ln/2. The value of m when you have only one pair of persons is $1/N$, because there are N possible dates. With n people, the mean number m is equal to the number of possible pairs divided by N, or $n(n - 1)/2N$. Setting this equal to ln/2, we see that n^2 must be approximately $2N \ln 2$, so $n \approx \sqrt{2N \ln 2}$. When $N = 365$, $n \approx \sqrt{2 \times 365 \times 0.693} \approx 23$.

The Long Run

Gamblers who make bad bets often get away with it and walk away as winners after a few bets. But in the "long run" they always lose. In fact, that might be considered a definition of the "long run"—it is enough trials to guarantee that a person who makes bad bets will lose. The number of trials required depends only on how bad the bets are.

Consider the colonel who was betting even money when the odds were 6 to 5 against him. He had a chance of 5/11 (about 45%) to win the first bet and walk away a winner. His chance of being ahead after five bets—his chance of winning three or more of the first five—was about 42% (as you can verify from the binomial distribution with $n = 5$ and $p = 5/11$).

After 125 bets, his chance of being ahead would have shrunk to 15%. Nevertheless, there was a modest chance that the colonel made a profit that evening. If that did happen, he may not know to this day how bad his bets were. But if he continued to bet that way on many occasions, the probability that he showed a profit is virtually nil.

Just how low that probability is can be deduced from the normal distribution. The chance of making money on a series of bad bets depends on the difference between the mean number of successes (m) and the number s that you need to have to make a profit. If the colonel made 1,100 bets, he would need 551 successes, but the mean m for this many bets is 500 (5/11 of 1100). The standard deviation in this case is about 17 ($\sqrt{500 \times 6/11}$), so the colonel would need a result that is three or more standard deviations above the mean. Table 2-2 gives the probability of such a deviation as only .00135.

As the number of bets increases, the standard deviation increases slowly, in proportion to the square root of n. But the deviation required to make a profit goes up directly with n. Quadrupling the number of bets, to 4,400, would make the required deviation 201 (m would be 2,000 and 2,201 successes would be needed), but σ would be merely doubled, becoming 34 instead of 17. So the colonel would then need a deviation of 6σ. Table 2-2 gives one chance in a billion for a deviation this large.

We see that, on a small number of bets, you can be lucky enough to get a result that falls on the right side of the normal curve. But when the number of bets is large, there is no right side; virtually the entire curve covers a range that results in a loss for you.

Table 2-3 shows the probability of bucking various house percentages and earning a net profit after various numbers of equal-sized bets. Knowing what you now know about the binomial (or normal) distribution, you could work out all these numbers for yourself. For example, when the "house edge" is 5% (approximately the edge in American roulette), your probability of winning each bet is .475. To win a net of $100 on 100 bets of $10 each, you must win 55 of those bets. The probability of doing this (or better) is 8.1%, but there is a 34.5% probability that you will lose $100 or more. The long run turns that little 5% edge into an insurmountable obstacle to profit.

You can see how minuscule are your chances of winning a significant amount after a large number of bets. Even when the edge is a mere 1.5%, after 400 $10 bets your chance of losing $400 is four times your chance of winning $400. And after a thousand bets against a house edge of 15%, your chance of winning anything at all roughly equals your chance of making the sea obey you.

In spite of these figures, you may have a friend who claims to have won money over the long run at the race tracks, where the house edge is more than 15%. He could be telling the truth if he knows more about the horses and the odds than the other bettors do. Although he can't beat the track, he can make money from the other bettors. But betting on unpredictable events like numbers at roulette is quite another matter, and the "systems" that are touted for winning at these games are pure garbage.

Some of these systems will be discussed in chapter 4. All of them are based on the idea that you can improve your chances by changing the size of your bets according to some formula. Such a method can rearrange your losses and oc-

Table 2-3. Chances of Various Wins or Losses after a Series of $10 Bets

Number of bets	House edge	Chance of losing at least:				Chance of winning at least:			
		$400	$200	$100	$10	$10	$100	$200	$400
100	1.5%	.0001	.040	.227	.520	.401	.147	.020	.00002
	5.0%	.0003	.080	.345	.656	.274	.081	.008	
	15 %	.007	.344	.729	.921	.053	.008	.0003	
400	1.5%	.049	.258	.440	.599	.363	.227	.106	.012
	5.0%	.171	.520	.709	.829	.147	.073	.025	.0016
	15 %	.856	.981	.995	.999	.001	.0002		
1000	1.5%	.224	.450	.575	.671	.306	.224	.141	.044
	5.0%	.636	.837	.903	.940	.053	.031	.0145	.0024
	15 %	.9997	.99998			.0000007			

casionally permit a large win in the short run, but none can possibly work in the long run.

To understand the certainty of this statement, consider the reason for varying the sizes of your bets. It is because you know that you will surely lose if the bets are all the same size. But a collection of bets of different sizes is made up of, say, a set of $1 bets, a set of $2 bets, a set of $4 bets, and so on. We know that your set of $1 bets, taken by itself, will lose. So will your $2 bets; so will your $4 bets. So how can you make a profit from the lot of them if each individual set of bets is a losing proposition?

The Drunkard's Walk

The results of a long series of trials can be represented as a "random walk," or "drunkard's walk." To play the role of drunkard, just take one step forward when the trial results in a success and one step backward otherwise. The results for a series of 2,000 actual trials with $p = 1/2$ are shown in figure 2-3. We can think of these as coin tossing, with "heads" being a success.

Notice that there were only three times when the number of heads equaled the number of trials—at the 1st, 3rd, and 250th trials. Since each of those trials resulted in a "success," the number of tails never exceeded the number of heads during the entire "walk." Such a result is not unusual; most people are surprised at the length of "runs" during which one side or the other remains ahead on such walks. When heads exceeded tails by 40 [at trial number 1,750], there was still no tendency for tails to catch up; tails fell another 24 behind on the next 190 trials, and ended the walk at 60 behind.

You will notice in figure 2-3 that there are many "streaks" where the curve climbs [or falls] continuously because of a series of consecutive heads [or tails]. Streaks are normal. Each time a head is followed by a tail [or vice versa], a new streak can begin. On 2,000 trials, this will happen an average of 1,000 times. Half of those times, the next toss will match the first one, to begin a new streak whose length is two or more. Half [250] of the streaks of length two or more will end at two; the other half will have a length of three or more. Extending this reasoning, we can deduce that, on the average, there should be approximately

250	streaks of length 2	125	streaks of length 3
62.5	streaks of length 4	31.2	streaks of length 5
15.6	streaks of length 6	7.8	streaks of length 7
3.9	streaks of length 8	2	streaks of length 9
1	streak of length 10	0.5	streak of length 11

and so on, on a series of 2,000 coin tosses. Of course we will never have a fractional number of streaks; the actual number of streaks of each length will be governed by Poisson statistics. For example, the probability of having *no* streak of length 10 is e^{-1}, and the probability of having no streak of length 11 is e^{-5}.

You can verify for yourself that the lengths of the streaks in figure 2-3 follow the above pattern quite well. In the first 1,000 trials, there was no streak of length 10, but there were two streaks of that length in the next 1,000 trials. Both of these occurrences have a reasonably high probability. The frequency of streaks is important in the analysis of betting systems, as we shall see in chapter 4.

© 1953 United Features Syndicate, Inc.

Figure 2–3. Random walk generated by 2,000 tosses of a coin. Dot goes up one unit on "heads" and down one unit on "tails."

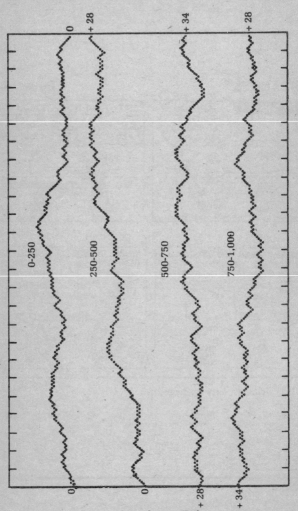

0-250

250-500

500-750

750-1,000

Excess of Heads over Tails

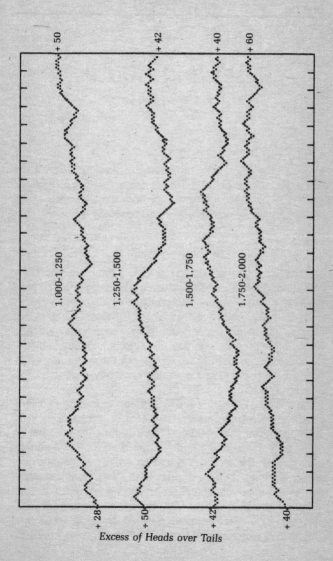

Excess of Heads over Tails

CHAPTER 3

Uses and Abuses
of Statistics

Now that we know how statistical distributions behave, we can look into the possibilities for using statistics to analyze events. We can also see how to protect ourselves from those who profit by the use of phony or misleading statistics.

Random Sampling

Polls are a part of our way of life. People are polled on everything from nuclear disarmament to preferences in peanut butter. But obviously the pollsters can't question everybody on every subject, so they take a "random" sample. For example, they might ask 3,000 New Yorkers whether they would be willing to, say, pay more taxes for improvements in the subway system. If 1,800 say yes, the poll reports that 60% of the population are willing to pay the higher tax for this purpose.

On the face of it, this seems absurd—to think that 3,000 people chosen [presumably] at random can accurately represent 8 million New Yorkers. But it is simply a question of how much accuracy is desired. Even if all 8 million people were polled, the accuracy would be limited by people who change their minds from one day to the next. So it is reasonable to shoot for something like an uncertainty of 2% or less on a poll of this sort—that is, to be able to say that between 58% and 62% of the population would say yes if asked.

It is also reasonable to set a 95% "confidence level" in

the result—that is, to be able to say that the probability is 95% that the result for the entire population lies between the quoted limits [58% and 62% in this case]. To estimate the confidence level, we refer to the normal distribution; there is a 95% probability that any given result is within two standard deviations of the mean. So if we want to have 95% confidence that our result is within 2% of the true mean, we must have a standard deviation that is equivalent to 1% of the sample. Let's see if that is true for the example given.

If p is 0.60 and $n = 3,000$ [the sample size], then the standard deviation is $\sqrt{1800 \times 0.4} = \sqrt{720} = 27$, which is just about 1% of 3,000. There is a 95% probability that the true value of p for the whole population lies between 1,746/3,000 and 1,854/3,000, or between 58.2% and 61.8%. Thus 3,000 people constitute an adequate sample.

Notice that the size of New York City does not enter into the calculation; a random sample of 3,000 is just as accurate for New York City as it is for Ottumwa, Iowa. But the diversity of New York's population creates a problem in obtaining a truly random sample. If we had a bin full of grommets, we could probably get a random sample just by sticking in a scoop and pulling some out. But if we scooped out people from New York City, the results of scooping them from Wall St. and scooping them from Harlem would be vastly different.

To account for the diversity of population, we could try to use a method that chooses each person individually at random without regard for individual differences. If you can figure out how to do that, you could make a fortune. But don't think you can do it with a telephone; it doesn't work. If everybody had a listed telephone, you could just take each name randomly from the phone book. However, that is a big "if." The telephone technique was thoroughly discredited when a highly publicized telephone poll predicted victory for Alf Landon over Franklin D. Roosevelt in the 1936 presidential election. Obviously, the people without telephones preferred Roosevelt.

So pollsters now try to match their sample to the population by adjusting it to have the same mix as the general population in terms of religious preferences, ethnic backgrounds, income levels, and whatever else they can think of. Obviously, they don't get a truly random sample that way, but it seems to work fairly well as long as enough of those polled are willing to give accurate answers. Don't trust a poll giving the percentage of men who patronize prostitutes or a poll of voters in Chicago. [According to Chicago newspaperman Mike Royko, a Chicago TV station once announced an hour before the polls closed that Bernard Carey was the winner of an Illinois election with "63% of the vote." Carey lost. Many Chicagoans had lied when asked whom they had voted for; in Chicago's "unique political atmosphere," they feared a "brick through their window."]

Random sampling has many uses other than in public opinion polls. Every drug or vaccine is subjected to a statistical test before it can be approved. Two random samples are used; one, the "control" sample, is given a placebo, and the other sample is given the drug to be tested. The researchers who analyze the results do not know which subjects were given the actual drug, so unconscious bias is minimized.

They then look at the difference between the number of people who improve after taking the drug and the number who improve after taking the placebo. For example, suppose 100 people are treated with the drug and 20 of them show improvement, whereas in the control group, 18 of 100 show improvement. For each group, the standard deviation is approximately 4, so it is highly probable that the drug is worthless.

If a control group had not been used, the 20% who were "helped" by the drug would refuse to believe that it is worthless. This is what leads to controversy when untested drugs are hailed as miracle drugs and then fail to pass a controlled test. The regulatory agencies are accused of suppressing lifesaving medicine for supposedly nefarious purposes when their real purpose is to save precious time [and money] for people who might be helped by other treatments.

Vaccines must also be evaluated statistically, but a vaccine for a rare disease presents problems because a large number of cases must be considered. Suppose a disease affects an average of 1 pig out of 100. If 100 pigs were inoculated and none contracted the disease, nothing would be proved. There was a probability of 37% (e^{-1}) that none of those pigs would have contracted the disease anyway. But if you inoculate 1,000 pigs, and 1 of them gets the disease, you can have confidence that the vaccine works. If the vaccine were ineffective, the probability that 1 or fewer of the pigs would get the disease would be only about .0005. [In this case Poisson statistics can be used, with $m = 10$, because p is so small.]

Situations involving rare events often become controversial because of the difficulty of gathering statistics. One controversy involves the effects of low-level "ionizing radiation" from nuclear reactors, X rays, and other sources. As a result of Hiroshima, Nagasaki, and later bomb tests, we know the probability of getting cancer from large doses of radiation; it is about .02 from a dose of 100 rems,[1] .04 from a dose of 200 rems, and .06 from a dose of 300 rems. It might seem from these figures that the chance of getting cancer is directly proportional to the dose, and therefore a dose of 1 rem would give a probability of .0002 of getting cancer. But this is an *untested* assumption because statistics cannot be obtained for doses of much less than 100 rems.

Suppose you wanted to measure the probability of getting cancer from a dose of 1 rem. If the probability were indeed .0002, we would need a population of 100,000 persons just to detect 20 cases from this cause, and we would need another population of 100,000 as a control. Since cancer might take many years to develop, we would have to follow these people for a long time; during this time, many of them would contract cancer for other reasons. Even if that many people were willing to be irradiated to set up this test, we would find that we were dealing with thousands of cases of cancer in each population. A difference of 20 cases would be less than one standard deviation and would not prove anything.

Interpretation of Statistics

Averages

The *mean* value, m, for a distribution is what we often call the "average." We find the mean value of a set of results by adding up all the results and dividing this sum by the number of results that we have. For example, suppose a small company were to pay its president $200,000 per year, its vice president $100,000, its secretary and treasurer $50,000 each, four of its employees $12,000 each, and the other eight eligible employees $10,000 each. The average, or mean, salary would be $528,000 divided by 16, or $33,000. This makes the company look very generous (and may make salaries look large compared to profits), but an employee is far below "average" unless he or she is an officer of the company. (I am not suggesting that any particular company has such a salary structure, but it is a possible way to disguise profits for public relations purposes.)

When a distribution is asymmetrical, as in this example, it may be more revealing to give the *median*. The median is the result in the middle, with just as many results above it as there are below it. In the above example, $11,000 is the median, with eight salaries above and eight below.

It is also useful to know the standard deviation. The average IQ is supposed to be 100; this is the mean as well as the median. But the fact that someone scores below 100 on an IQ test does not mean that this person's overall intelligence (whatever that is) is below average, even if IQ scores are a good measure of "overall intelligence." The same person can score 103 (above average) on one day and 98 (below average) on another day. The standard deviation in a given person's score is about 3 points; that is, if a person's IQ is 100, there is a 68% probability that he or she will score between 97 and 103 on any given IQ test.

The standard deviation in the scores of the whole population is of course larger; it is about 13 points. So 68% of the population scores between 87 and 113, and a score of 140 puts someone in the top 0.1% of the population—at least in the ability to do well on IQ tests.

When considering subgroups of the population, we may find that the average IQ differs from 100. For example, Lower Slobbovians may have an average IQ of only 94. If the distribution is normal, about 30% of them would score above 100 and 10% above 110. This might tell us something about educational policy. Even if you assume that someone with an IQ of 94 cannot profit from higher education, it would be a mistake to conclude that Lower Slobbovians, *as a group*, cannot profit from it. It would be ridiculous to deny an educational opportunity to a Lower Slobbovian with an IQ of 110 just because his group, for whatever reason, has an average IQ of 94. [This is not the place for a discussion of the significance of IQ tests for members of minority groups, but that is also an important consideration.]

The Detached Statistic

"Of those tested, 67% preferred ultralite Burpo beer to Olde Frothingslosh." What does this commercial mean? Nothing at all, for several reasons:

1. What do you care what other people prefer? It's what you like that counts.
2. Maybe Olde Frothingslosh was the only beer that people liked less than Burpo.
3. How many results did they ignore before doing this test?
4. Does 67% mean 67 out of 100, or two out of three?

Of course we know better than to believe a TV commercial. But what about our own government "of the people, by the people, and for the people." They wouldn't use meaningless statistics to sell us something—would they? Try this example.

According to testimony of the Department of Transportation [DOT] before the U.S. Congress, an automobile is more energy efficient than a passenger train for intercity travel. But according to testimony by the DOT [that's right, the same agency], the train is three times as efficient as the auto! Both assertions were backed by authentic-looking figures, carried out to four-digit "accuracy."

In the first testimony, the fuel efficiency of the train was taken to be the average for the whole Amtrak fleet (including many inefficient locomotives and "political" trains that carry few passengers), but the second testimony was based on the efficiency of new turbo-charged diesels with modern light-weight cars. Which statistic would you rely on if you had to make a decision on whether to buy new rail equipment?

To compare with the auto, it was assumed that each car carries an average of 2.6 people in intercity travel. This is a classic case of a "detached statistic"; that is, it has no relevance to the question it was supposed to address: "Do you save energy by replacing autos with trains?" The people who take the train are not "average." An Amtrak survey showed that 63% of rail passengers were traveling alone, 22% were with one companion, and only 15% were in a group of three or more. If 100 of these people had traveled by auto, there would have been about 63 one-person cars, 11 two-person cars, and 4 or 5 cars to carry the others—a total of 78 or 79 cars for 100 people, or about 1.3 people per car. If the train carried 260 passengers, it replaced 200 autos, not the 100 suggested by the "average" of 2.6 per car.

The discrepancy between these figures can make us wonder how the DOT got the number of 2.6. I did my own survey of people in intercity autos on five occasions (in Kentucky, Ohio, Pennsylvania, Maryland, and Tennessee), and I found between 190 and 210 people in 100 cars on each occasion. You don't have to take my word for this any more than you should take the word of the "experts" in Washington; try it yourself and let me know what you find. (My results were obtained on weekday afternoons; you might find a larger number on weekends when more families are traveling.)

We are only concerned with the validity of quoted statistics here, so we have not attempted to account for all the hidden energy costs in transportation. But the red herrings uncovered here are of general interest, and they point out the difference between "average" cost and marginal cost. Unless you are prepared to construct (or dismantle) an entire system, the average cost has no relevance to any decision. It is the cost of an additional unit—the marginal cost—that counts.

The Spurious Digits

The above-mentioned DOT testimony quoted an energy consumption of 2,837 British thermal units (Btu) per passenger mile for the average auto in intercity traffic, compared to 3,123 Btu per passenger mile for the "average" train. These numbers are reminiscent of the museum guard who proudly told visitors that the dinosaur bones on display were "60,000,005 years old." When asked how the age could be known so precisely, the guard said, "I don't know how they do it, but when I started work here five years ago, they told me that dinosaur was 60 million years old."

Similarly, the quotation of energy consumption to four digits implies an accuracy that just isn't there. The uncertainty in each figure must be several hundred, because variations in occupancy and energy efficiency from one vehicle to another lead to uncertainties of 10% or 20% in each figure that goes into the calculation.

It is customary and logical to assume that quoting a figure as 2,837 means that the figure is not 2,847 or even 2,838. If the uncertainty is in the hundreds, then it should be rounded off to 3,000 and stating it as 2,837 is not being accurate—it is being dishonest. The implied accuracy says that vehicles consuming "3,123" Btu are definitely less efficient than the ones consuming "2,837," when in fact the opposite might be the case.

A classic example of the use of irrelevant digits occurs in the TV series "Star Trek" when Mr. Spock reports to Captain Kirk something like, "We now have 117.53 seconds until the engines blow up." If he wanted to maintain the illusion of accuracy, he could at least have said, "At the sound of the tone, we will have 117.53 seconds until the engines blow up; beep." [It is reliably reported that a Vulcan can make a "beep" sound in less than .01 second.]

Statistics in Science and Pseudoscience

Science makes predictions about the world. It tells us that, if we do "this," we will observe "that." If we slam a proton into another proton at a certain speed, we will produce a lambda particle X percent of the time.

Science can also make predictions about human beings. If a group of people receive a whole-body dose of 500 rems of radiation, 50% of them will die within a few days or weeks. This prediction is not as precise as the previous one, however, because all protons are identical and no two people are identical. But in a sufficiently large random sample, the prediction is verifiable.

Pseudoscience also makes predictions, but never in a quantitative way. It will say that there are certain "influences" that give people certain "tendencies." If pseudoscience were real science, we could do a statistical test, comparing people who are exposed to these "influences" with people who are not. But somehow, this is never possible with pseudoscience. Objections are raised to all controlled tests, and there is never any proof that these influences even exist, let alone have the effects that are claimed for them. We can wonder in vain how these influences were ever "discovered" in the first place.

However, some scientists have attempted to apply the methods of science—statistical analysis—to the claims of pseudoscience. Let's look at some of the results.

Astrology

Astrology deals with "influences" of the sun, moon, and planets on human behavior. One influence is the Sun Sign—the sign in which the sun "resides" when a person is born. Other influences include the "Ascendant"—the sign that is rising when someone is born—and the positions of the planets at the moment of birth.

Some might say that all of this is a harmless diversion, not worth a scientific test because nobody really believes it. But a teacher, writing in a professional journal, suggested that students be grouped by astrological Sun Sign.[2] Public libraries carry astrology magazines giving advice on choosing a mate by the Sun Sign. None of this is marked "For amusement only." So it seems worthwhile to see if there is anything about it that can be verified.

A scientist, confronted with a situation in which numerous claimed influences may conflict with one another, will try to simplify the situation by doing a controlled test on only one influence. Because the Sun Sign is easy to determine, it is ideal for such a test.

You might object that "serious astrologers" themselves scoff at the astrological advice, based entirely on the Sun Sign, that is given in newspapers and magazines. But all astrologers claim that the Sun Sign has an "influence." Linda Goodman, the "world's greatest astrologer,"[3] says the Sun Sign is "easily the most important single consideration" in "analyzing human behavior."

How do you test an "influence?" Suppose you were charged with developing a program to influence school children so that more of them would study science and eventually become scientists. Years later, how would you test to see if you had, in fact, exerted the desired influence?

The most unbiased test would be to look in a directory of scientists to see how many of your proteges had actually achieved something in science.[4] You would also look up a control group of people who were not exposed to your influence but who were otherwise similar to your own group. If the directory listed significantly more of your proteges than your "controls," you could say that your program had an influence. If it did not, you'd have to report that your program failed to influence people in their choice of occupation.

The same study can be made of astrological influences. Statements of many astrologers[5] testify to the effect of the Sun Sign on choice of occupation [or aptitude for an occupation, which certainly is tied up with success in an occupation].

Table 3-1 shows the results of a test in which 16,634 birthdates were chosen from consecutive listings in *American Men of Science* [1965 edition]. The mean number m for each sign is 1,222. If $p = 1/12$ for each sign, then according to

Table 3-1. Number of Scientists' Births by Sun Sign

Sign	Dates (inclusive)[a]	Births	Proportion in general population[b]
Capricorn	Dec. 24 - Jan. 19	1,241	0.992
Aquarius	Jan. 23 - Feb. 18	1,217	1.025
Pisces	Feb. 21 - Mar. 19	1,193	1.022
Aries	Mar. 23 - Apr. 18	1,158	0.989
Taurus	Apr. 23 - May 19	1,185	0.978
Gemini	May 24 - June 19	1,153	0.993
Cancer	June 24 - July 20	1,245	1.015
Leo	July 25 - Aug. 20	1,263	1.036
Virgo	Aug. 25 - Sept. 20	1,292	1.038
Libra	Sept. 25 - Oct. 21	1,267	0.998
Scorpio	Oct. 25 - Nov. 20	1,246	0.962
Sagittarius	Nov. 24 - Dec. 20	1,202	0.949

a. To avoid effects resulting from shifts in the boundaries (leap year effect), only the central twenty-seven dates for each sign were used.

b. Proportions in the general population were deduced by Guy Le Clercq (of the Cosmoplanetary Research Institute, Brussels) from *Le Mouvement Naturel de la Population dans le Monde de 1906 a 1936*, by Henri Bunle.

SOURCE: Data in columns 2 and 3 are from John D. McGervey, "A Statistical Test of SunSign Astrology." *The Skeptical Inquirer*, Summer 1977, table 1. Reprinted in *Paranormal Borderlands of Science*, edited by K. Frazier (Buffalo, N.Y.: Prometheus Books, 1980). Copyright 1980 by Prometheus Books. Reprinted by permission.

the normal distribution, the standard deviation should be $\sqrt{(11/12)} \times 1,222$, or 33.5. Notice that only two of the twelve numbers are (barely) more than two standard deviations from the mean; one is high and one is low.

In reading a few astrological works, I have found four signs that were mentioned more than once as being "favorable" to science. These are Aquarius, Gemini, Virgo, and Sagittarius.[6] The total number of births under these four signs is 4,864—an average of 1,216, or ten fewer than average for the "control" group (the other eight signs). If each number is corrected for seasonal variations in the birth rate, as shown in the last column of table 3-1, the total becomes 4854, or an average of 1214.

Of course, if you play with these numbers long enough, you will find some grouping for which the total number of birthdays is two or more standard deviations above the mean. [Given enough random numbers, you can always do that.] And you could probably find some astrology book that would call these signs favorable to science in some way.

But if you think that such a manipulation would "support" astrology, then I would like to make you a substantial wager. There are about 100,000 names in *American Men of Science* [later called, more accurately, *American Men and Women of Science*]. Decide which signs have been "shown" to be favorable to science, and let us then test your findings on another 20,000 or so names taken from consecutive listings. If we find a corrected excess of 5% or more for your "favorable" sign[s], I'll pay off.

There have been other studies of this sort, using more specific categories of occupation, and no significant excess for the allegedly favorable signs has ever been found. This does not "disprove" astrology, of course. If you tell me that you have an invisible animal in your basement, it would be hard for me to *prove* that you are wrong. But when people make that sort of claim, the burden of proof is on the claimants.

Biorhythms

The idea of biorhythms seems plausible until you see what the pseudoscientists have done with it. Numerous living organisms, as well as humans, exhibit cyclical behavior, or "rhythms." But the known rhythms in humans are changeable; we can recover nicely from jet lag in a couple of days.

On the other hand, proponents of biorhythms assert [without telling us how they found out] that [1] there are three fixed rhythms, or cycles, whose periods are exactly twenty-three days, twenty-eight days, and thirty-three days, respectively, [2] these cycles have exactly the same period in every human being, and [3] these periods begin at the moment of birth and never change in length.

An easily testable component of biorhythm theory is that "critical" days occur when any of the three cyclic curves crosses the zero axis, which happens twice in each period for each cycle. On such days an individual is more likely to perform erratically and to have accidents. Proponents cite studies [mostly undocumented] that found about 60% of accidents caused by human error occurred on critical days.

Let's suppose that accidents occur at random. There are twenty-one noncritical days in the first cycle, twenty-six in the second, and thirty-one in the third. So the probability that a day chosen at random is not critical on any of the three cycles is [21/23] × [26/28] × [31/33], or 79.6%. The probability that a random accident occurs on a critical day is thus 20.4%, and a finding that 60% of accidents occur on such days would be highly significant in a moderately sized sample.

A study by T. Williamson[7] did show that 27 out of 46 aircraft accidents occurred on the pilots' critical days. Since the expected number, 20.4% of 46, is only 9, the result appears to be unquestionably significant.

But Williamson gave away the fallacy when he said, "Days considered to be critical are the calculated critical days plus or minus one" [to allow for individuals born close to midnight].[8] This provides six critical days instead of two for each cycle, and it makes the overall probability that a day is not critical equal to the product [17/23] × [22/28] × [27/33], or 47.5%. "Critical" days of this type become 52.5% of all days! [This is not three times the percentage computed previously, for now there are more instances of a critical day's falling on a critical day from another cycle.]

The mean number of accidents on Williamson's critical days should therefore have been 52.5% of 46, or about 24, if the accidents are randomly distributed. The observed 27 has no significance. There have now been many tests by unbiased observers to determine whether there is a correlation between accidents and critical days. Over 25,000 accidents have been examined, and no biorhythm effect has appeared.[9]

Other tests have focused on sports performances. For example, no biorhythm effect was found in the occurrence of 100 no-hit baseball games between 1934 and 1975, or in the occurrence of 1051 record sports performances.[10]

So the only real biorhythm effect is the transfer of money from the pockets of the gullible to those of the promoters. You can even buy an electronic biorhythm calculator.

The Lunar Effect

Werewolves! Moon goddesses! Lunatics! With such images, Dr. Arnold Lieber introduces his "open-minded" study of the effect of the lunar phase on human behavior.[11]

No one can deny the possibility that the moon affects human behavior. But Dr. Lieber was not content to find explanations that might involve only the *light* of the full moon. He decided that the effect should be gravitational and related to the tides. Such an effect would occur at the time of the *new* moon as well as the full moon—that is, whenever the tides are higher than normal.[12]

Having decided this, he did a statistical study. From the coroner of Dade County, Florida, he obtained the dates and times of 1887 homicidal attacks that had occurred over a fifteen-year period, and he plotted the number of attacks per day vs. the number of days from the new moon. He found what he was looking for—a "peak" at the full moon and another peak that he described as being at the new moon (but which actually was two days after the new moon; see table 3-2).

Lieber then "confirmed" this result by doing a similar statistical study of 2,008 homicides in Cuyahoga County, Ohio, that had occurred over a thirteen-year period, 1958–1970. His "confirmation" showed a peak two days after the new moon, another peak three days after the full moon, and a third peak (which he ignored) nine days after the full moon. Hmm.

Lieber interpreted the three-day shift at the full moon as a newly discovered "latitude effect." But he failed to explain

Table 3-2. Frequency of Homicides on Days of the Lunar Cycle

Day of attack	Dade County[a]	Cuyahoga County	
		Lieber [1958–70][a]	Sanduleak [1971–81][b]
1 [new moon]	43	57	119
2	65	64	120
3	82	83	122
4	58	77	111
5	68	65	121
6	64	64	106
7	62	64	119
8	66	60	103
9	59	57	126
10	72	60	135
11	69	69	104
12	64	69	105
13	71	72	104
14	55	51	125
15	62	59	121
16 [full moon]	86	66	100
17	54	52	124
18	63	77	102
19	71	88	117
20	67	57	126
21	49	69	118
22	59	67	119
23	60	67	108
24	70	60	108
25	53	86	108
26	64	74	116
27	68	53	94

[table continued on next page]

Table 3-2. continued

| Day of attack | Dade County[a] | Cuyahoga County | |
		Lieber [1958–70][a]	Sanduleak [1971–81][b]
28	51	77	104
29	57	75	118
30	54	81	127[c]

a. Numbers measured from the graph in Arnold L. Lieber and Jerome Agel, *The Lunar Effect* [New York: Doubleday, 1978].

b. Sanduleak numbers [not previously published] were tabulated by him from data kindly provided by the Cuyahoga County coroner's office.

c. The Sanduleak study covers 136 lunar periods. In 64 of the periods, the new moon occurred on the thirtieth day, and events on such days are tabulated with day 1 [the next period]. The number of homicides, for the 72 times when the thirtieth day was not the new moon, was 67; the number would be 127 if the same average were maintained for 136 dates.

why the new-moon peak fails to show the same shift or why his introduction cited strange behavior in New York and Philadelphia [nearly the same latitude as Cleveland] on nights when the moon was full, not three nights later. Conclusion: Lieber took great latitude with the data.

Many scientists feel that such distorted interpretations of data, made to fit claims that are based on no known physical laws, should be challenged. One such scientist is Dr. Nicholas Sanduleak, an astronomer at Case Western Reserve University in Cleveland [Cuyahoga County], Ohio. He decided to examine the Cuyahoga County records for 1971–1981, the years following the ones that Lieber studied. His results are shown in table 3-2, alongside those of Lieber.

Notice that there are no conspicuous peaks anywhere in the 1971–1981 results. The high point comes at day 10, nowhere near either the full moon or the new moon. But even without this study, it is clear from Lieber's own data that nothing significant occurred. Notice that no peak anywhere exceeds three standard deviations, and also notice that many deviations just as large as the ones Lieber calls "confirmation" are simply ignored (without explanation). Furthermore, the occurrence of the Cuyahoga County peak three days after the full moon is not a confirmation that weird behavior occurs on nights of the full moon.

The statistical study of homicidal attacks was the centerpiece of Lieber's book. His anecdotal references to strange behavior are as reliable as gamblers' reports of big winnings. People remember strange behavior when there is a full moon, just as they remember their gambling winnings (and forget their losses).

Sanduleak's study did show a correlation of attacks with the day of the week, with a big peak on Saturday night. (That's why they call it a "Saturday-night special.") One can imagine a hospital attendant on a busy Saturday night saying, "There must be a full moon tonight!" But how often does anyone check that out? If they do check it later and find that the moon was not full, do they go back and tell everybody?.

Summary

We have seen that some understanding of statistical fluctuations can help us to see through the fog that often drifts in from people who are intent on proving a particular point. All data are subject to random errors and statistical fluctuations. Beware of those who claim that some fluctuations are significant and others are not on the basis of a theory that "prejudiced" scientists fail to believe.

The purveyors of hokum may express outrage at the way their theories are dismissed, but they are laughing all the way to the bank. The truth never catches up with the fable, partly because of the public's lack of understanding of what constitutes reliable data.

CHAPTER 4

Betting Systems

Gambling "systems" are a fertile field for exploring the principles of probability and statistics. Two kinds of strategy are commonly employed by gamblers. The first, the winners' strategy, is to seek out propositions in which the mathematical expectation (discussed in chapter 1) exceeds the amount bet and to risk money only on such propositions. People who "gamble" in this way include bookmakers, racetrack operators, casino operators, and expert cardplayers. These people are not really gambling; in the long run they are sure to make a profit. In succeeding chapters we shall see some of the methods they employ to make sure that their expectations are adequate.

The profits made by these winners are achieved at the expense of people who pursue the second kind of strategy. The second strategy involves compounding a series of losing propositions in the hope that a winning proposition will emerge. For example, these people might use some arithmetical system to decide when to bet, and how much to bet, at roulette.

In chapter 5, I show that the house percentage in American roulette is about 5%. This means that, in the long run, the bettor would be just as wealthy (poor) if the house, instead of going through with each bet, simply returned to him $.95 out of each $1 that he bet. The futility of trying to add up five-cent losses to come out with a profit should be obvious. But arithmetical systems still flourish, and some books present them as reasonable methods. Therefore it is useful to examine the fallacies of a few of them in detail.

Balancing

This is an absurdly simple system based on the principle of the "maturity of chances," or the "law of averages." Unfortunately, this "law," as it is popularly conceived, does not exist. The theory (if you can call it that) of this system is that you should bet on outcomes that are "overdue" because the number of times that each result appears should eventually catch up to the expected "average." For example, if a coin comes up heads five times in a row, you should bet on tails because the number of tails should soon start to catch up to the number of heads.

The random walk shown in figure 2-3 of chapter 2 vividly shows the fallacy of this kind of reasoning. Half of the "streaks" shown there end on the next trial and half continue, no matter how long the streak has lasted up to that point. This must be so because *the coin can't remember how it came up before.* In fact, after a long streak of heads, you would be better advised to bet on heads because of the possibility that it is a two-headed coin.

People bet on the basis of hazy memories of past experiences. They remember that it is unusual for a coin to come up heads six times in a row, and therefore they bet against that result. They seem oblivious to the *reason* why six heads in a row are unusual: to get six in a row, they must get five in a row first. Once they already have five in a row, the probability of getting another head is one-half, as always.

Unfortunately, some otherwise reasonable books contribute to the confusion on this point. A book by an author of dozens of books on games says, "The difference between the number of heads and tails thrown tends to decrease as the number of tosses increases." If that were true, then balancing would be a reasonable method. But just the opposite is true. The difference between the numbers tends to increase even though the percentage difference decreases. This is clear from the Pascal triangle (chapter 1), simply because it *is* a triangle that gets wider as n, the number of trials, increases. It is also clear from the normal distribution (chapter 2) in which the standard deviation increases as n increases.

"What I can't understand—
why doesn't *everyone* just keep doubling their bets?"

Drawing by Richard Decker. Copyright © 1944, 1972 by The New Yorker Magazine, Inc.

The point is that a coin has no memory. Thus it cannot possibly compensate for any imbalance between the past number of heads and tails; it can only dilute it. Eventually this dilution causes the percentage of heads to approach 50%. For example, after a streak of 5 heads in a row, if 100 additional flips gave you the expected 50 heads, you would have a total of 55 heads on 105 flips, for 52.5% heads—not an unusual percentage. It is not unusual to get 10 more than the average number of heads on 100 coin tosses; it would be very unusual to get 10 more than average on 20 tosses; and it would be impossible to get 10 more than average on 19 tosses.

The balancing system does have one advantage. People using it refrain from betting while they wait for a streak to develop in order to bet that it will end. Any system that saves you money by making you bet less often can't be all bad.

The Martingale

The martingale system guarantees that you will have a profit if you keep on betting long enough. The catch is that the system itself ensures that you can't keep betting long enough, because it calls for doubling your bet after any losing bet. Sooner or later a losing streak will prevent you from placing the required bet, either because it would exceed the house limit or because you are broke.

The success promised by the martingale is based on making each bet larger than the sum of all preceding losing bets, so that a winning bet always recoups all losses and provides a profit equal to the size of the first losing bet. For example, if your first bet is $1 and you lose four bets in a row, you will have lost $1 + $2 + $4 + $8, or a total of $15. Your next bet will be $16, giving you a $1 profit if you win it.

Success with the martingale is achieved only by exposing yourself to great risk. If you start with a mere $1 bet and your bankroll is $1,023, you will be wiped out if you lose ten bets in a row. You will lose $511 on your first nine bets and $512 on the tenth one. The probability of losing ten bets in a row is quite small, but by committing yourself to this series of bets, you are in effect betting $1,023 to $1 that it won't happen.

If each bet had a 50% chance of success, the probability of losing ten bets in a row would be $(1/2)^{10}$, or $1/1024$, and the odds would be 1023 to 1 in your favor. But in practice, with the house edge at work, the odds in your favor are far less. A bet on, say, "red" in roulette has a probability of $10/19$ of losing. Thus losing ten in a row would have a probability of $(10/19)^{10}$, which is about $1/613$. On 613 trials, you should expect to win $1 on 612 occasions and lose $1,023 on the other occasion.

If you still have some lingering doubts, look at the random walk (figure 2–3). Suppose you were betting on heads and you had a bankroll of $1,023. After 1,000 trials, betting $1 each time at even money, you would be $28 ahead, having won 514 bets and lost 486. The martingale would have done much better; it would have recouped all the money you lost on the 486 tails and left you $514 ahead—$1 for each head. But continuing the martingale would have led to disaster; starting at the 1,377th trial, you would have lost ten in a row, for a loss of $1,023. At this point you would have a net loss of $309, leaving $716 in your pocket—not enough to bet the necessary $1,024 on the next trial. If you then started all over again with a $1 bet, you would recoup $11 before you would begin, on the 1,410th trial, a losing streak of nine in a row. At the end of that streak you would have a mere $216 and a net loss of $807.

Obviously (if the house limit permitted it), you could have avoided disaster this time by starting with a bankroll of $2,047. But eventually you would encounter a losing streak long enough to wipe that out, too. And remember that this example did not allow for any house percentage. If you were betting on "red" at roulette, each set of thirty-eight bets would give you an average of only eighteen wins instead of nineteen. Take every nineteenth "head" in figure 2-3 and change it to a tail; then see how well your martingale works.

In describing the martingale and related systems, one book on gambling says, "The player must have enough of a bankroll to withstand temporary losses." Unfortunately, you have no way of knowing that a loss will be "temporary." Losses are losses, and after any loss, the odds on future bets still favor the house. The larger your bankroll, the larger the profit—for the casino.

The 1–3–2–6 System

Unlike the martingale, this system tells you what to do after a winning bet. It is a sequence of four possible bets, which is terminated if the player loses a bet. Beginning with a bet of one unit, the player (if he wins that bet) next bets three units. If this wins, he reduces his bet to two units (keeping a profit of two units), and if he wins again, his final bet is six units. After any loss, the player starts again at the beginning of the sequence (until he goes broke).

There are five possible outcomes of a sequence:

A: First bet loses; player loses one unit.
B: Second bet loses; player has a net loss of two units.
C: Third bet loses; player has a net profit of two units.
D: Fourth bet loses; player breaks even.
E: Fourth bet wins; player has won a total of twelve units.

Gullible people who believe in a free lunch might say, "There are five possibilities; only two lose, and two win. The wins are bigger than the losses, so the system must work." You know better. The argument fails because the possibilities are not equally likely. If the house has no edge at all, each bet has a 50% chance of winning. Therefore outcome A is 50% probable; B, 25% probable; C, 12.5%; and D and E, each 6.25%. You can work out for yourself that the player just breaks even under those conditions (as he would no matter how the bets are varied in size). Naturally, when the house has an edge, the edge prevails and the player loses.

The Reverse Martingale

The 1–3–2–6 belongs to a class of systems in which the player increases his bet after a *win* instead of a loss. In contrast to the martingale, which produces many small wins and an occasional devastating loss, the 1–3–2–6 and its cousins yield a large number of small losses and a small number of large gains. Systems like the latter are highly touted by people who claim great success with them, because they remember their large wins and they forget how many small losses they suffered.

The purest form of such a system is the "reverse martingale," which calls for constant bets after each loss, but doubling of the bet after each win. This method provides an occasional spectacular success at the expense of many small losses. It is popular with players who believe that the dice or cards "get hot," and their memorable successes lead others to try it. Unfortunately, the dice never know that they are "hot"; they continue to give the same probabilities on each throw, occasionally producing a streak that may end at any moment.

Whether or not the dice are hot, everybody agrees that no streak goes on forever, so the player must decide how large a win will satisfy him. [Or the house limit may decide this for him.] Let us suppose that a roulette player, betting on "red," decides to play a reverse martingale by letting each win "ride" [thereby doubling his bet] until he wins seven times in a row [seven being a well-known magic number]. Each time he has a winning streak that stops short of seven, his total loss is just equal to his original bet since the additional amounts that he bet were "house money" that he won during the streak. If his initial bet is $10, he wins $1,270 [$10 + $20 + $40 + $160 + $320 + $640] when a streak reaches seven. But the probability of winning each bet is only 9/19 [see chapter 5], making the probability of seven wins in a row equal to $(9/19)^7$, which is about 1/187. So on 187 starts, he figures to have one streak of seven that will win him that $1,270, and on the other 186 occasions he will lose $10, for a net loss of $590 [$1,270 minus $1,860].

What is this player's chance of taking home a profit of $1,000 or more? To do this, he would need to win his $1,270 before he loses more than $270, which means he needs to succeed on one of his first twenty-eight attempts. Since the probability of success on each attempt is only 1/187, we can use Poisson statistics [chapter 2] with the mean number of successes being 28/187 [about .15]. The probability of no success is then e^{-15}, which is about $1 - .15$, making the probability of at least one success about .15. If this happens and he takes his money and goes home, he will be able to talk about it for a long time.

It is interesting to use table 2-3 to compare the results of a reverse martingale with the results of a series of equal bets when the house edge is 5%. The table shows that the chance of winning $200 or more after 100 $10 bets is only .008. On the other hand, playing the reverse martingale with $10 initial bets, a player will be $200 ahead if he has a five-win streak (probability 1/42) in his first twelve bets, or a six-win streak (probability 1/89) in his next thirty-two bets, or a seven-win streak (probability 1/187) in his next sixty-four bets (counting a whole series as a single bet until a loss occurs).

From Poisson statistics, the probability of no five-win streak in twelve tries is $e^{-12/47}$, of no six-win streaks in thirty-two tries is $e^{-32/89}$, and of no seven-win streaks in sixty-four tries is $e^{-64/187}$. The combined probability that no streak will occur soon enough is the product of these numbers, which works out to only a 37% probability that the player will fail to win $200.

So the reverse martingale seems to be sensationally effective in producing large wins. However, when the required streak fails to show up, the player has lost $10 on each of 108 tries, for a total loss of $1,080. In effect, all the reverse martingale does is to raise the stakes. If your goal is to win $200, why not just bet $200 all at once? You would have a better than 47% chance of winning and you could lose only the $200. Curiously, some people make a distinction between this type of bet and the larger bets made during a reverse martingale. They say the latter bets, made during a winning streak, are made with "house money." But money is money. Before you let that money "ride," it belongs to you, not to the house; you could take it home and pay the rent with it.

Cancellation

Finally, here is a system that would hardly be worth mentioning except that some people have a childlike faith in it. To follow the cancellation system, you write down the numbers one through ten in a vertical column and then bet as many chips as the sum of the top and bottom numbers. IF you win, you cross off the top and bottom numbers; if you lose, you write the amount lost at the bottom of the column. You then bet the sum of the new top and bottom numbers and repeat the same procedure.

When you have crossed off all the numbers, you have won the total of the original numbers—in this case, fifty-five chips. Each time you win you cross off two numbers, and when you lose you cross off only one number. So you should surely be able to cross off all the numbers eventually, shouldn't you? Unless of course you go broke after losing a series of steadily increasing bets, as in the simple martingale. Try this system with the "random walk" of chapter 2 and see how you do. [To simulate roulette, change every nineteenth "head" into a "tail" and bet on "heads."] The casino operators have never barred anyone for using this system; that should tell you something.

Conclusion

We see that these systems do nothing more than change the stakes or rearrange the losses. Why do people believe in them? It may simply be that they want to believe that they have some control over the outcome of their gambling. But how can people continue to believe when the systems fail, as they must?

There are two reasons for this: First, they don't keep careful records, and they remember wins longer than losses. Second, very few people are disciplined enough or careful enough to follow a system perfectly; when they lose, they blame it on their own failure to follow the system, and the system is then exonerated. But we know better. We know that no system can add up a series of losing propositions and produce a profit.

CHAPTER 5

The House Percentage

Your everyday life may not include a visit to a casino, but you have many other opportunities to participate in organized gambling. The purpose of this gambling is to help out your local church, state government, or friendly neighborhood bookie. If you participate with that in mind, you will achieve your goal. But if you have any idea that you might strike it rich, forget it. You'd have a better chance in a casino.

In this chapter I discuss the house percentages in the various games that you can play, both in and out of a casino, and we'll see which, if any, gives you the best chance for a windfall.

Charities and Rackets

The difference between a charity and a racket is in the use to which the money is put. The similarity is that both, when running a gambling operation, collect a very high house percentage. Let's see how they manage it.

Lotteries

It would be impossible to list, let alone analyze, all the different forms of lotteries that are running these days. Most states run them, as do private charities. But lotteries have one thing in common—they return very little of the money to the players as prizes. Playing your state lottery is just a way to make a voluntary contribution to your state government. With all the grumbling about taxes, it is surprising that so many people are willing to contribute in this way, and it is unfortunate that the people who can least afford it are the biggest contributors.

One reason for the popularity of these sucker bets may be simply the convenience of being able to buy a ticket at the corner store. But psychological tricks also play a part. Here are a few of them:

1. The operators offer more than one way to win. Each ticket may have several potential winning numbers, or several prizes may be drawn in a raffle. Even though each way of winning is about as easy as striking oil in your backyard, the mere fact that several ways exist is bait enough for some people.

2. They change the rules frequently, either devising new ways to select the winner or changing the prizes [giving out no more total money but just distributing it differently]. This may bring back people who have quit because they had been steady losers.

3. They make the prizes sound bigger than they really are. A prize may be listed as $300,000, but what you get is $15,000 per year for twenty years. I hear you saying you wouldn't mind winning either one, but there really is a big difference. If you actually won the $300,000, you could pay the taxes on it, invest what was left, and get an annual income of well over $15,000, while keeping the principal intact indefinitely.

There is nothing more to say about most lotteries. No strategy can be used to improve your chances, and the house edge is so high that you should simply avoid them except as a way of contributing to charity. But even with their huge house edge, some lotteries have offered rare opportunities for smart bettors. The method used to beat such lotteries is instructive.

In these lotteries, which were run by some European countries, the bettor had a choice of five numbers, which he selected by marking a card containing the numbers 1 through 90, arranged as shown in figure 5-1. First prizes went to players whose five numbers all matched the five numbers

Figure 5-1. Lottery ticket showing five numbers
chosen by a player.

1	✗	3	4	5	6	7	8	9	✗
✗	12	13	14	15	16	17	18	19	20
21	22	23	24	25	26	27	28	29	30
31	32	33	34	35	36	37	38	39	40
41	42	43	44	45	46	47	48	49	✗
51	52	53	54	55	56	✗	58	59	60
61	62	63	64	65	66	67	68	69	70
71	72	73	74	75	76	77	78	79	80
81	82	83	84	85	86	87	88	89	90

SOURCE: H. Steinhaus, *Mathematical Snapshots*, 3d ed. [New York: Oxford Univ. Press, 1969]. Reprinted by permission.

drawn by the lottery officials. The first-prize winners shared equally in 15% of the total amount bet. Players with four winning numbers split another 15% of the pot, as did those with three and those with two. The remaining 40% was the house edge, going to the government.

The chance of matching five out of five was $[5/90] \times [4/89] \times [3/88] \times [2/87] \times [1/86]$, less than 1 in 40 million; the chance of matching four was about 1 in 100,000 [you can work this out yourself], and the chance of matching two numbers was about 1 in 44. No matter how "smart" he was, a player couldn't change these probabilities; nobody could predict which numbers were more likely to be drawn.

But that didn't matter. What mattered was that the smart players could maximize their expectation by picking numbers that gave a bigger payoff when they did win. Obviously, the payoff depended on how many other players picked the same numbers; a player who picked unpopular numbers was in a position to collect more if he won. Not too surprisingly, certain numbers were unpopular; people tended to avoid numbers at the edges and corners of the card.

Maybe they were thinking of the card as a "target," which receives more hits near the center. But whatever they were thinking, the effect was big enough to take advantage of. A study of four thousand tickets provided by one lottery office showed that the corner numbers were selected only about half as often as the average.[1] A player who picked corner numbers therefore had an expectation at least twice as large as the average 60 cents on the dollar, and in this way he or she actually overcame the enormous house edge with ease.

Winning at Lotto

Human beings always have prejudices like those displayed in avoiding corner numbers, and one can sometimes take advantage of these prejudices in other lotteries—for example, in the "lotto" game now running in many states. In this game, one selects a set of numbers—six numbers from 1 through 40 in the Ohio game—and the winners share a pot consisting of a fixed percentage of receipts. If human prejudice causes six particular numbers to be played only 80% as often as the average, then a player who selects all six of those numbers will have more than double the expected return, and he will thus come out ahead in the long run. I'll leave it to you to determine which numbers are unpopular in your state.

Picking the unpopular choice is profitable in any gamble where the pot is divided among the winners. The outstanding application of this strategy occurs in racetrack betting, discussed in chapter 7.

Bingo

Bingo is a form of lottery that is popular because it gives the players a place to go to socialize and also gives them some control over their destiny. The players lose money, of course—that's the purpose of the game—but inattentive ones lose more money.

One gimmick that appears in bingo games is worth calculating. Sometimes a special prize is offered for filling the entire card by the time forty-eight numbers are drawn. There are seventy-five possible numbers, and you need twenty-four numbers to fill the card, so you might think you have a fighting chance. To calculate how big your chance is, divide the seventy-five numbers into two groups—the forty-eight that are drawn and the twenty-seven that are not drawn. The probability that any given number on your card will be in the "drawn" group must be 48/75. Assuming that this number is drawn, then there will be forty-seven numbers left in the drawn group out of a total of seventy-four. Thus, the probability that a second given number will also be drawn must be 47/74. Working through all twenty-four numbers, we see that the probability that all will be drawn must be [48/75] × [47/74] × [46/73] × . . . × [25/52]. Multiplying all twenty-four factors gives a probability of 1/799,399.

In what was billed as the "world's biggest bingo contest," in Cherokee, North Carolina, a prize of $200,000 was offered to any player who could fill a card by the forty-eighth number. There were 2,400 players who paid $500 each for three bingo cards. Most of them bought additional cards, so the total number of cards was perhaps as high as 30,000. With each card having a probability of 1/800,000, there was a probability of only about 3/80 that the prize would be claimed, and it was not. However, the drawing continued, with a prize of $100,000 for the first player to fill a card. Six players divided the prize, having succeeded on the fifty-third number.

You can work out for yourself the probability of six successes on the fifty-third number. It is a rather unlikely occurrence.

The Numbers Game

The true odds in the numbers game are easy to compute. There are 1,000 equally likely numbers—000 through 999—so your probability of winning on a single number is 1/1,000. If your $1 bet is a winner, you will be paid $500. If all numbers are bet equally, the operators take in $1,000 for each $500 paid out, for a house percentage of 50%.

Of course the numbers racketeers collect that 50% in the long run even if certain numbers are more popular than others, because they have a 50% edge on each number. But they want to be sure to show a profit on every single day, and therefore if a certain number is too popular, they cut their risk by reducing the payoff on that number.

One popular option is to "box" three numbers. This means that you win if these numbers come up in any order; for example, 123, 132, 213, 231, 321, and 312 would all pay off if you boxed 1, 2, and 3. This bet gives you six chances instead of one, but because it pays only one-sixth as much when you win, the house percentage is still 50%.

If you bet the numbers daily, as some poor souls do, you will win about once in three years and consider yourself very lucky. But you would have contributed twice as much as you "won"; you would be far luckier if you had never heard of the game. The only winners are the operators and the people who sell those little "dream books" telling you which number has been "predicted."

The fact that you can choose your own numbers provides a certain attraction—so much so that many states now have a numbers game in their lottery package. Alas, the states are no more generous than the mobsters; their house edge is also 50%, but they still get customers.

Casino Games

A casino can be an extremely exciting place, with action at all hours, a plush layout, crowds swarming around the winners, and big-name entertainers. You can enjoy this at a very modest price as long as you are careful and don't lose your head. You might even come home with some of the house's money if you are disciplined and you do your homework.

But casinos can be hazardous to your financial health, especially if you have a good credit rating, because [unlike other forms of entertainment] casino gambling can cost you an almost unlimited amount of money—in a single evening—if you let it. So before you start, set aside the amount you are willing to lose to pay for that evening's entertainment. Then, when you have lost that amount, QUIT. Trying to "get even" can lead to disaster; the dice, the wheel, and the cards [after shuffling] have no memory and no compassion for a loser.

Remember that the casino operators are not gamblers. They have no intention of giving you the winning side of any proposition, and they know what they are doing. In the words of one operator, "When a lamb goes to the slaughter, the lamb *might* kill the butcher, but *we* always bet on the butcher."[2] Every game, no matter how small the house edge, reliably fills the role of butcher for the operators. The survival of the casinos is proof of that.

Keno

Keno is similar to the national lottery described at the beginning of this chapter. The player marks up to twenty numbers on a card containing eighty numbers. The house then draws twenty numbers, and the player wins if enough of his numbers are drawn by the house. However, in contrast to the national lotteries, keno has a payoff that is fixed in advance. Thus there is no way to gain by picking unpopular numbers, and the expectation for each type of bet can be computed.

Because there are several ways to win on each card, players have the illusion that they have a decent chance. For example, on the popular "eight-spot ticket," costing $.60, you win $5 if five of your eight numbers are drawn, $50 if six are drawn, $1,100 if seven are drawn, and $12,500 if all eight are drawn. That sounds good until you calculate the player's chances of winning.

The probabilities are computed as we did for the bingo jackpot. The probability that any one of your numbers will be drawn is 20/80. Given that this number is drawn, the probability that a second one will be drawn is 19/79, and the probability that all eight will be drawn must be [20/80] × [19/79] × [18/78] × [17/77] × [16/76] × [15/75] × [14/74] × [13/73], which equals 1/230,115. To find the probability that seven of eight will be drawn, we replace the factor

Table 5-1. Expectations on a Sixty-Cent, Eight-Spot Keno Ticket

Number of hits	Probability	Payoff	Expectation [probability times payoff]
5	.018303	$5	$.0915
6	.0023667	$50	$.1183
7	.000160455	$1,100	$.1765
8	.0000043457	$12,500	$.0543

13/73 by 60/73 (because there are sixty numbers in the "undrawn" group) and we multiply by 8 (because there are eight sets of seven numbers that can be selected out of the eight numbers you have chosen). This and the other probabilities are listed in table 5-1.

The expectation for each way of winning is also shown in the table. Adding these together gives you a total expected return of $.4406. This leaves the house with a profit of almost $.16, or 27% of your sixty-cent bet. There are other tickets— "one-spot," "two-spot," etc.—with a similar house edge (20% or more), making keno one of the biggest sucker bets in Nevada. It ranks behind only craps, blackjack, and nickel slot machines in casino revenue.

Slot Machines

The "one-armed bandit" is well named. Like other games with a big house edge, it lures the pigeon by offering many different ways to win. But when these ways are all added up, you are lucky if the machine returns $.75 for each dollar dropped in. If you think you can improve on this return by exercising "skill" to control these mechanical marvels, you probably also check under your pillow to see what the tooth fairy left you.

To figure your expectation on any particular machine, you have to compute the expectation for each possible way of winning, as we did for keno. For example, on a machine analyzed by Professor Philip G. Fox of the University of Wisconsin,[3] there were the usual three dials with twenty positions on each dial, making a total of $20 \times 20 \times 20$ or 8,000 different combined positions at which the dials could stop. The maximum payoff was sixty-two units for three bars. There was one bar on dial 1, three on dial 2, and one on dial 3, making 3 possibilities out of 8,000 to win those sixty-two units and giving you an expectation of $.0233 on the dollar. There were nine other winning combinations of symbols, which added another 1,166 ways to win, but these brought the total expectation up to a mere $.736 on the dollar.

Chuck-a-Luck (Birdcage)

Chuck-a-luck, like other high-profit games for the house, is popular because it gives several different payoffs. These are artfully chosen to create the illusion that the house edge is quite small.

The game is played with three dice, contained in a sort of double birdcage shaped like an hour glass. This container is rotated to throw the dice onto the floor of one cage. A player can bet on any number from one to six. If his number appears on one die, he collects at even money; if it is on two dice, he is paid 2 to 1, and if it is on all three dice, he gets 3 to 1.

Suppose $1 is bet on each of the six numbers. If the dice show three different numbers, the house breaks even, collecting on three numbers to pay off the other three. If one number comes up on two dice, the house collects $4 from the four losers, pays $2 to one winner and $1 to the other, and keeps $1. If the same number is on all three dice, the house collects $5 and pays out only $3. The house edge comes out to 7.87%.

This house edge is computed as follows. The probabilities are:

- All three numbers different: $[5/6] \times [4/6]$, or 20/36
- All three numbers the same: $[1/6] \times [1/6]$, or 1/36
- Two numbers the same: 15/36

With $1 bet on each number, the house makes $2 with a probability of 1/36 and $1 with a probability of 15/36, for an average profit of 17/36 of $1. Dividing by the total bet of $6 gives us 17/216, or a percentage of 7.87% for the house.

In spite of this house edge, a friend of mine once told me that he could beat this game consistently. I don't recommend his method; I just report it for your amusement. It depended on the fact that, in one casino at least, the dice did have a "memory." He noticed that the operator would simply turn the cage upside down for each play and that this could allow one of the dice to fall straight through without turning over. It would then land showing the face that was opposite to the one it had just shown [1 is opposite 6, 2 opposite 5, and 3 opposite 4]. He maximized his chances by waiting until the same number appeared on all three dice, then betting on the opposite number. He claims to have walked away a winner from eleven straight sessions. On his twelfth visit, the owner plied him with drinks until he found out the secret of this success, and of course the opportunity vanished.

Roulette

Betting on the spin of a wheel is a very old form of gambling. The idea of combining the ball with the wheel is credited to Pascal [who did not use it for gambling] in the seventeenth century. In the European version of the game, the player has a reasonable chance. There are thirty-seven pockets in the wheel, numbered zero through 36, but players bet only on 1 through 36 and are paid off at odds that would be correct for a wheel containing no zero. Thus, on the average, the house breaks even when the ball lands in numbers 1 through 36, but it collects 100% when it lands in zero. This makes the house edge 1/37, or 2.70%. American casinos do better by having a double zero as well as a zero pocket. They still pay off as if there were thirty-six pockets, and thus they collect 2/38 of the money bet, or 5.26%.

There are a variety of bets to make, but none of them reduces the basic house percentage [although some increase it]. Since 36 is exactly divisible by 2, 3, 4, 6, 12, and 18, you can bet on combinations of two numbers, three numbers, four numbers, six numbers, twelve numbers, and eighteen numbers, with payoffs of 17 to 1, 11 to 1, 8 to 1, 5 to 1, 2 to

1, and even money, respectively. Because all of these would be the true odds for a wheel containing thirty-six pockets, the house edge remains at 5.26% for all such bets. But there is also a five-number combination for people who wish to make a larger donation to the house. This bet pays 6 to 1, which would be correct for a wheel containing only thirty-five pockets, so the house edge on this bet is 3/38, or 7.89%.

Craps

For a small bettor who can't invest the time and effort required for learning the best blackjack strategy (chapter 6), craps is the best bet in a casino (as long as he avoids the optional sucker bets that the house offers). The house edge on a bet that the shooter will "pass" is a mere 1.41%. Stick to that kind of bet, and your money will last for a reasonable length of time.

To compute the house percentage, let's look at table 1-1. The probability that the shooter will "pass" equals the probability that he will roll a 7 or an 11 on his first roll, plus the probability that he will "make his point" after rolling an initial 4, 5, 6, 8, 9, or 10. (The shooter's "point" is what he rolls on the first roll; to make his point, he must roll that number again before rolling a 7.) These events are mutually exclusive, so we can add the probabilities as follows:

- Probability of 7 or 11 = 1/6 + 1/18   = 2/9
- Probability of 4 or 10 times probability of making point = 3/18 × 3/9   = 1/18
- Probability of 5 or 9 times probability of making point = 4/18 × 4/10   = 4/45
- Probability of 6 or 8 times probability of making point = 5/18 × 5/11   = 25/198
- Total probability = 2/9 + 1/18 + 4/45 + 25/198   = 244/495

So the odds against a pass are 251 to 244. The house offers even money and therefore wins $251 and loses $244 for a profit of $7 on every $495 bet. This makes the house edge 7/495, or 1.414%.

The house also lets you bet on "don't pass," but of course it won't give you the 251 to 244 edge. Your "don't pass" bet is canceled if the shooter's first roll is a 12 (which would win for you if you were the house). The 1/36 probability of this result must be subtracted from the overall 251/495 chance for "don't pass," leaving you a winning probability of 949/1,980. Your chance of losing is still 244/495, or 976/1,980. On 1,980 bets of $1 each, the house wins $976 and loses $949, for a net profit of $27 on the $1,925 in noncanceled bets (fifty-five bets are canceled). The house percentage is thus 27/1,925, or 1.403%, almost the same as on a "pass" bet.

But be careful if you bet this way! Some houses may elect to cancel "don't pass" bets after a roll of 2 instead of 12, and this doesn't change the house edge. But others may cancel on both 2 and 12, reducing your winning chance by another 1/36, to 894/1,980. The odds against the player then become 976 to 894, and the house edge is thus a nice fat 82/1,870, or 4.39%.

You may be curious about the effect that the 1.4% house edge has on a martingale. If there were no house edge, you know that the odds would be 1,023 to 1 against losing ten bets in a row. The odds against losing ten "pass" bets in a row are of course smaller. The probability of losing each bet is 251/495, so the probability of losing ten in a row is $(251/495)^{10}$, which equals about 1/890. That tiny 1.4% edge has reduced the odds from 1,023 to 1 down to 889 to 1.

At a typical crap table the house averages far more than a 1.4% profit because the players fall for an astonishing variety of sucker bets. There is no need to discuss all of them; there are only two that give the house an edge of less than 4%. One is a "place bet" on 6 or 8. A place bet on any number is a bet that the shooter will roll that number before he rolls a 7. The house gives the following odds on place bets:

- Odds of 9 to 5 for bets on 4 or 10 (house edge 6.7%)
- Odds of 7 to 5 for bets on 5 or 9 (house edge 4.0%)
- Odds of 7 to 6 for bets on 6 or 8 (house edge 1.5%)

You should be able to verify the quoted house percentages for yourself. For example, if you bet $6 on 8 or 6, you get back $7 plus your original $6 when you win. The probability of winning is 5/11, so your expectation is 5/11 of $13, or $5.91. The house keeps an average of $.09 on each $6 bet, so the percentage is 1.5%.

Place bets give rise to yet another idiotic system. This one calls for making all six place bets simultaneously, giving you odds of 4 to 1 in favor of winning one of them. [There are twenty-four ways to roll one of the place bettor's numbers, and only six ways to roll a 7.] Assuming that you win one of these bets, you then cancel the others. But a loss means a loss on all six bets.

Suppose you bet $6 on each of the six numbers, and each number wins the expected number of times during a series of fifteen bets. You will lose three bets, totaling $108; you will win five bets on 6 or 8, for $35; four bets on 5 or 9, for $33.60; and three bets on 4 or 10, for $31.20. Your net loss will be $8.20—just one more reminder that you can't add losses to give a profit.

The other exceptional side bet at craps [giving the house an edge of less than 4%] is offered to you after you have made a pass bet. If the shooter "comes out" on a point [that is, his first roll is 4, 5, 6, 8, 9, or 10], you can make an additional "point bet" at the true odds. This bet, that the shooter will make his point, can be for any amount up to the size of your original bet. The only catch is that the house will not pay off odd cents to winners of these bets. For example, a $2 point bet on 9 will pay off $3, but a $1 bet will only pay $1. So there is no point to a point bet of less than $2 on 5 or 9, or less than $5 [at 6 to 5 odds] on 6 or 8. If you want to be able to make the maximum possible point bet at true odds, your original pass bet has to be for $10.

The house will generously let you make a point bet for an amount larger than your original pass bet, provided that you also increase that original bet to the same amount. You won't fall for that, will you? The original bet still pays off at even money, but the odds against winning it have risen considerably.

Baccarat

This is a relatively new card game in U.S. casinos, and the rules are somewhat complicated. However, the player has no choice in what to play, so you don't need to know any rules—you just have to be able to bet.

You can bet on either the "bank" or the "player," each of whom is dealt two cards initially. Either of them may get one more card, strictly on the basis of the rigid rules that are posted; neither has any option in the matter. Following these rules, the bank wins 50.68% of all hands, exclusive of ties. Bets on the player pay off at even money, so the house has a 1.36% edge [50.68% minus 49.32%]. Bets on the bank are paid off at odds of 19 to 20 [the bettor is returned $39 on a $20 bet], making the house edge only 1.17% on bank bets. [On 10,000 $20 bank bets, $39 is returned to the player 5,068 times, for a total of $197,652, leaving the house $2,348 out of the total $400,000 bet.]

Because the player has so little choice in baccarat, except to decide how much to bet, the game is a breeding ground for the arithmetical systems that we debunked in chapter 4. The high minimum bet makes the martingale obviously impractical, but "modified martingale," the "1-3-2-6," and "cancellation" systems are all touted. Because the small house edge allows the users of these systems some successes, people who should know better continue to recommend them. Edwin Silberstang,[4] in a book on baccarat, says, "Astute players have a plan and stick to that plan, and if the betting method is valid, they will end up winners."

Poppycock. It is simply dishonest to assert that any "plan" [that is, arithmetical system] can make you a winner when the house has the edge on every single bet. Using any system, or using no system, you will occasionally win, but in the long run you lose.

Hitting It Big

Table 5-2 summarizes some house percentages for games we have discussed in this chapter. Notice one feature: the games offering larger odds also have a larger house edge. The reason is easy to figure—supply and demand. More people like the thrill of big odds, so they pay a premium to get it.

If a big hit is what you crave, you can try for it without paying such a large premium. Simply use the reverse martingale on a low percentage game. For example, instead of betting $1 on the numbers, try to win $512 by betting $1 at craps, intending to let it ride until you have won nine bets in a row. The odds against winning those nine bets are only 581 to 1 at the crap table, compared to 999 to 1 against hitting a number. Either way, you have risked only $1 of your original money.

Table 5-3 compares your chances of winning at least $500, while risking only $1 of your own money, for several popular games. The surprising result here is that, on this kind of gamble, roulette is a better bet than craps even though its house edge is almost four times as large. Why? Because at roulette you can reach your goal of $500 in only two bets. First, you bet your $1 on a single number. If you win you get $36, which you then bet on a two-number combination, picking up 18 × $36 for a total of $648 (including your original dollar) if you succeed. Your probability of winning both bets is (1/38) × (1/19), or 1/722, making your expectation $648/722, or $.898. If you play for nine successive passes at craps, your expectation is $512/582, or only $.88.

Remember that roulette is still a poor choice for a single bet. It works out better in this situation because you make fewer bets than you would at craps. On the other hand, maybe you don't want to make fewer bets; maybe you gamble for the fun of making a lot of bets. In that case, stick to the low-percentage games and avoid roulette.

Table 5-2. Summary of House Percentages

Game	Type of bet	Payoff odds	True odds	House percentage
Keno	Eight-spot 8 hits ticket	62,500 to 3	230,114 to 1	27.0
	7 hits	5,500 to 3	6,231 to 1	
	6 hits	250 to 3	421 to 1	
	5 hits	25 to 3	54 to 1	
Chuck-a-Luck	Any 3 hits	3 to 1	215 to 1	
	2 hits	2 to 1	201 to 15	7.87
	1 hit	even	47 to 25	
Roulette	Single number	35 to 1	37 to 1	5.26
	Two-number combination	17 to 1	18 to 1	5.26
	Three-number combination	11 to 1	35 to 3	5.26
	Four-number combination	8 to 1	17 to 2	5.26
	Five-number combination	6 to 1	33 to 5	7.89
	Six-number combination	5 to 1	16 to 3	5.26
	Twelve-number combination	2 to 1	13 to 6	5.26
	Eighteen-number combination	even	10 to 9	5.26
Craps	Pass [come]	even	251 to 244	1.41
	Don't pass [don't come]	even	976 to 949	1.40
	Place bet [6 or 8]	7 to 6	6 to 5	1.52
	Place bet [5 or 9]	7 to 5	3 to 2	4.00
	Place bet [4 or 10]	9 to 5	2 to 1	6.67
	Big six or big eight	even	6 to 5	9.09

Cheating in Casinos

Obviously, the probability that a gambling house is cheating can't be computed mathematically, but certain circumstances make it more probable. Thorp said that against one dealer he lost twenty-four blackjack hands out of twenty-six (with one win and one tie). When you compute the probability that this can happen without cheating going on, you must conclude that cheating was highly probable.

Table 5-3. Chances of Hitting It Big

Game	Type of bet	Payoff on $1	True Odds	Expectation
Numbers	Single number	$500	999 to 1	$.50
Roulette	Single number, let winnings ride on two-number combination	$648	721 to 1	$.898
Craps	Ride until nine successive wins	$512	581 to 1	$.88
Chuck-a-luck	Ride until eight successive wins	$576 or $864 [usually]	1007 to 1	$.519

People have too readily dismissed the possibility of cheating in a legal casino with the bland assertion that the house figures to be honest because it can make money without cheating. But that doesn't prevent cheating in other businesses. The trouble is that the house can make more money if it does cheat, and greed is the basis of all gambling.

Console yourself with the fact that not all dealers know how to cheat, and the ones who do command more pay, so if you don't attract attention you are likely to get an honest deal. The house brings out the cheaters mostly to "get even" with players who are winning "too much." If you ever are in that position, be ready to make a quick exit.

CHAPTER 6

Blackjack

Blackjack deserves a separate chapter, for it has at last provided gamblers with a system that worries the casino operators. In response to Edward O. Thorp's computer-tested system, many casinos changed their rules.[1] But not many people are willing to work hard enough to make the system pay off, and the changes in rules were so unpopular that the blackjack tables were losing business. So some of these changes were rescinded, allowing the casinos to fleece the suckers at the usual rate but permitting the diligent player to make a profit (until he or she is thrown out of the place).

The Basic Strategy

Figure 6-1 shows the rules deduced from the probabilities reported by Thorp. If you learn only these rules (even ignoring the exceptions listed there), you will be within 1 percent of an even game against the house (without varying the size of your bets or counting cards). If you master the exceptions, you will draw even. If, in addition, you count the cards in order to make larger bets in favorable situations, you will have the edge over the house (even if you count only tens and multiple decks are used).

I shall assume that you already know the basic rules of the game that apply at all casinos. But casinos differ in many details, particularly in the options for doubling down, splitting pairs, and buying "insurance." Each additional option provides possibilities for finding a profitable situation, so

Figure 6-1. Basic blackjack strategy.

A. *Standing and Doubling Down.* Stand on numbers shown and on all higher numbers. Double down only on numbers shown. "Soft" totals are those in which an ace is counted as 11. All other totals are "hard." Note exceptions below table.

Card shown by dealer:	Two or three	Four, five or six	Seven or eight	Nine or ten	Ace
Stand on hard total of:	13	12	17	17	17
Stand on soft total of:	18	18	18	19	18
Double down on hard total of:	9, 10, 11	9, 10, 11	10, 11	11	11
Double down on soft total of:	17	13 through 18	—	—	—

Exceptions:
1. Double down on hard 10 vs. dealer's nine.
2. Double down on soft 18 vs. dealer's three.
3. Double down on five-three or four-four vs. dealer's five or six.

B. *Splitting Pairs.* General rules are (with exceptions below):
1. Always split aces and eights.
2. Never split fours, fives, or tens.[a]
3. Split other pairs only if dealer shows two through seven.

Exceptions:
1. Split nines vs. eight or nine, but not vs. seven.
2. Split fours vs. dealer's five.
3. Split sevens vs. dealer's eight.
4. If rules do not permit doubling down after splitting, then do not split the following: fours vs. five, threes vs. two, twos or threes vs. three.

a. Throughout this chapter, "tens" include face cards, which count as 10 points in blackjack.

casinos that restrict such options should be avoided. Let us take a look at each option.

Insurance

If the dealer's top card is an ace, a player may make an "insurance" bet of up to one-half of his original bet. If the dealer's other card is a ten (giving him a "natural" or "blackjack"), the player wins his insurance bet at odds of 2 to 1. A player who is "fully insured" wins enough on insurance to compensate for losing his main bet to the dealer's blackjack. Even if the player has no ten, the forty-nine unseen cards (in a freshly shuffled single deck) contain only sixteen tens and thirty-three non-tens, so the odds against the dealer's having a blackjack are 33 to 16, and insurance is a bad bet.[2] But if you have already seen some other cards, and have been counting tens, it could be a different story.

Doubling Down

After all "naturals" have been settled, a player may double his original bet and take exactly one additional card. In some casinos this option is restricted to hands originally totaling 11, or totaling 10 or 11. Most players would not double down on other totals anyway, but figure 6-1 shows that you should sometimes double down on 9, or even 8 or "soft" 18. Preventing you from doing this must work to your disadvantage.

Splitting Pairs

If a player's first two cards are a pair, he may split them into two hands. His original bet goes on one hand, and he draws at least one card to each hand. If aces are split, the player can draw only one card to each ace, and a total of 21 no longer counts as a natural. On other splits, some casinos let the player double down after drawing the first card to either hand; this slightly increases the player's chances. Some casinos also permit any two ten-value cards to be split as a pair—for example, a king and a queen could be split, a strange move that sometimes pays off.

Some of the advice in figure 6-1 seems quite strange to people who have absorbed the folklore of blackjack, but its correctness is backed up by detailed figures in Thorp's book. For example, it seems peculiar to stand on a total as low as 12; but when a dealer shows a four, five, or six, this is clearly the best strategy. When dealer shows a five, and you stand on 12, you win 43% of the hands. Not too good, but the alternative is worse; if you draw, you win less than 41% of the hands.

This is not the place for a detailed discussion of all blackjack strategy. That requires a whole book, and Thorp has already written it. But it is interesting to look at the odds in special cases in which Thorp's advice runs counter to advice found in other books. One well-known "guide to successful gambling," published quite some time after Thorp's book, said a player should "never, never" split twos, threes, fours, fives, or sixes because it is "simply throwing good money after bad. If you split you will simply have two worse hands with twice as much money invested in them."

This is nice rhetoric, but it has no basis in fact. It is no wonder that casinos still make money on blackjack with advice like that being published. In certain situations, following that advice could cost you $.27 on each $1 bet! When you hold a pair of sixes against the dealer's five, and you split the sixes, you stand to win $.17 per dollar bet; if you don't split, your best action is to draw, but that stands to lose you $.10 on $1.

The reason for the big difference is that a total of 12 is miserable; starting with 6 is much better. Drawing a six through a ten gives you 12 through 16, no worse than you had before. Drawing anything else puts you in a good position, and if you are then allowed to double down you are riding high. If doubling down is not permitted after a split, your profit on these splits is cut by about $.06 on $1, but it is still well worth it to split sixes.

You don't have to take all these computer results on faith. You can deal a few hundred hands (they go quickly) and test them for yourself. I tested splitting sixes vs. the dealer's six by removing three sixes from the deck and dealing 1,200 hands. On 400 hands, I stood on the sixes, and I lost 239 of these hands. At $1 per hand, that's a loss of $78, or $.195 per hand (with a statistical standard deviation of about $.036). On the other 800 hands, I split the sixes (making my total "bet" on these hands $1,600), and I then followed the basic strategy for doubling down, drawing, and standing. My net profit on these hands was $79, or about $.10 per hand. So splitting gained me about $.30 per hand, very close to what Thorp's figures show.

Occasionally a book will tell you that you can't trust a system developed by a mathematician with a computer, that an experienced gambler's advice has to be better. The only way to judge such statements is by an actual test; don't take anything on faith, no matter how good the writer's claimed results are. So I put the following disagreement to the test, and you can do the same.

The gambler's book advises splitting tens [destroying an excellent total of 20] if the dealer shows a five or a six. On the other hand, Thorp's figures say that [betting $1 per hand] you win an average of $.674 and $.697, vs. 5 and 6, respectively, if you stand, but only $.521 and $.543, respectively, if you split.

To resolve this disagreement, I removed two tens and a five from a deck and then dealt 1,000 hands. On the first 500, I stood on the 20. I won 405 and lost 52, for a net win of $353, or $.706 per $1 bet. On the other 500 hands, I split the tens. I won 607 of the split hands and lost 326, for a net win of $245, or $.49 per initial $1 bet. These results are in excellent agreement with Thorp's figures. Apparently the author who scorned Thorp's results never actually tried such a controlled test. [Notice that no judgment is called for in this test. The dealer's action is controlled by the rules, and the player will always stand on his total of 12 through 21, after splitting and receiving one card on each hand.]

The above discussion is based on the assumption that the hands are dealt from a single complete deck. If, as often happens now, several decks are shuffled together, there is no change worth mentioning in the recommended basic strategy, and the game remains at almost a zero edge for the house. [The house edge is 0.2% with two decks and 0.4% with four decks.] This is still the best game in the house for you, as long as you are willing to learn the system.

Card Counting

Many stories have been told about the success of card counters at blackjack. A popular myth is that the use of multiple decks has wiped out the advantage gained by counting, but that is only partly true. Although multiple decks do reduce the number of advantageous situations for card counters, these situations still develop, and they persist longer than they would with a single deck.

The card counter gains any obvious advantage on insurance bets. We have seen that insurance is a bad bet if you do it without regard for any count of the cards. But if you can observe and count just a few of the other cards, you can bet only when the odds favor you; that is, when the ratio of non-tens to tens, among the unseen cards, falls below 2 to 1. Whether you yourself have a natural is immaterial; all that matters is the count.

To take full advantage of counting the deck, you must of course adjust your strategy on each bet according to the count at that time. This means varying the size of your initial bet, as well as changing your strategy on drawing, splitting pairs, and doubling down. We mention here only the simplest ideas, based on counting tens and non-tens. This alone can make you a winner instead of a loser (in the long run).

Any time the ratio of non-tens to tens is below 2.0, the player has the edge, even if he plays the basic strategy. Therefore you should increase your bets when that happens in order to make up for the losses when the house has the edge. To do this without attracting undesirable attention (and possible expulsion), you can simply let one or two wins "ride"—as if you were trying a reverse martingale, a system that never worries the operators.

To gain the best advantage from your count, you should modify the strategy in figure 6-1 when the ratio of non-tens to tens falls below 20. The most important modifications are:

1. When the ratio is 2.0 or less,
   a. stand on 12 vs. dealer's two or three, and on 16 vs. ten,
   b. double down on 8 vs. five or six.
2. When the ratio is 1.5 or less,
   a. stand on 16 vs. nine, and on 14 vs. ten,
   b. double down on 8 vs. three or four,
   c. split tens vs. two through six, nines vs. seven or ace, fours vs. three or four.

The complete strategy described by Thorp covers many more exotic possibilities, such as doubling down on as little as 5 when the dealer shows four, five, or six and the ratio is 1.0 or less. [The reason for this is not hard to see; with a deck so rich in tens, the dealer's four, five, or six puts him well on the way to a bust.] There are also strategies involving the counting of fives, or the counting of all cards. But enough is enough; some of these strategies are simply impractical for the average person unless he is tied into a computer while he is playing. I wouldn't want to gamble on getting away with that at a casino.

This raises the question of what you can get away with at a casino. The owners now know that winning systems exist, so if you are using one and they find out, the game is over. It is best to be inconspicuous. Do not make sudden large changes in the size of your bets, do not stack your chips so it is obvious that you are winning, and do not make it obvious that you are counting cards.[3]

At least, don't do what a card counter named Junior did [according to Thorp]. From his count, he knew that the one card remaining to be dealt was an ace, so with two tens he asked to double down—on a $200 bet! The dealer couldn't believe it, and tried to talk him out of it, as did the "pit boss" when he overheard the argument. Finally Junior lost his patience and yelled, "Give me the goddamned ace!" The card was dealt. Junior got his ace, his $400 profit, and an escort to the door, with an invitation never to come back.

CHAPTER 7

Horse Racing

Betting on sports events is one of our most popular pastimes. The spicy feature of these gambles is the element of choice. You may be at the mercy of blind chance (or a fix), but it doesn't feel that way. You always think that next time you will correct your mistakes because you have learned how to "pick 'em." I don't know if anybody really knows how to pick 'em, but you can use the principles shown here to get a better return when you pick the right horse.

Betting systems abound at the races (most of what I have to say also applies to dog races). Some bet on the jockey (not at the dog races, of course), and others on the horse's track record. Many will tell you that the temperature and track conditions are all important. Some like the long odds provided by various parlays; others claim a steady profit by betting on the sound horse to show.

But the most logical bettor of all was Hazel, the wife of my friend Paul, who had the system for chuck-a-luck. On one of the rare occasions when Paul took Hazel to the races, Hazel asked him which horse she should bet on in the first race. Paul was amused by the question. "You don't bet on every race," he explained. "This is a race for two-year-old maidens [horses that have never won a race]. There is no way of telling which one will win; they all have the same chance." Hazel concluded, logically, "If they all have the same chance, I might as well bet on that 50 to 1 shot." She collected a $100 profit on her $2 bet.

Hazel had the right idea. She maximized her expectation by picking a bet with a high potential return and a reasonable chance of success. But how can you tell what is reasonable? All sorts of people at the track are willing to help you out, but if they're so smart, why don't they have money of their own to bet?

Betting Pools

The answer lies in the huge house percentage, which is guaranteed by the method that is used to compute the payoffs. The standard bets are "win," "place," and "show." From the total amount bet in each of these categories, the track skims about 15% "off the top" to cover its share plus taxes. (So the only sure way to win is to buy the race track.) The remaining 85% in each category forms the "win pool," the "place pool," and the "show pool," respectively.

The Win Pool

This pool is divided among the bettors on the first-place horse in direct proportion to the amount bet by each of them. For example, if a total of $12,000 had been bet on various horses to "win," the win pool would be $10,200 (85% of $12,000). Say that $5,100 had been bet on Bug Juice, the winner. The $10,200 returned to the backers of Bug Juice would amount to twice their original bets, or a $4 return on each $2 bet (an "even money" payoff).

The Place Pool

This pool is slightly more complicated. Suppose that the place pool were also $10,200 in this race, with $5,100 (coincidentally) bet on Bug Juice to "place" and $1,020 on Crabgrass to "place." This money would be returned to the respective bettors, leaving $4,080 still to be divided. That amount would be divided into two equal parts, $2,040 for the Bug Juice backers and $2,040 for the Crabgrassers. The Bug Juicers' total payoff would then be $5,100 plus $2,040, or $7,140. This works out to $2.80 for a $2 bet. The Crabgrass partisans would get back a total of $3,060 on their $1,020 total bet, or $6 on a $2 bet.

The Show Pool

This is distributed in a similar way. After the track takes its 15%, the money bet on the first-, second-, and third-place finishers is set aside in separate lots. One-third of the remaining money is added to each lot, which is then parceled out to each successful bettor in proportion to the amount he or she bet.

It sometimes happens that the amount bet on the first three horses to show is more than 85% of the total show bets on the race. In this case there is a "minus pool," and the track is required to forego its usual 15% [or even take a loss] in order to return at least $2.10 on every $2 bet.[1]

Breakage

The track usually makes more than its nominal 15% cut because it rounds off all payoffs downward to the nearest multiple of $.20 per $2 bet. For example, if a computation like the one above called for one group of bettors to receive $2.56 per $2 bet, the track would pay only $2.40. The reason given for this is that the track doesn't want to deal in small change,[2] but the rounding applies even to $100 bets. When $2.56 is rounded down to $2.40, the payoff on a $100 bet is $120, and the track makes another $8. The extra money that the track makes on this "breakage" brings its overall percentage up another two or three points, to more than 17%.

Trends in the Betting

To overcome the huge "house edge," you have to do more than just pick winners. Anybody can buy a racing form and get advice from expert handicappers, who are about as successful as possible in picking winners at each track. But if you bet on the "consensus" choices of these handicappers, you'd lose your money rapidly.

Table 7-1 shows the returns on the consensus picks reported in newspapers over a two-month period in 1978. The first choices won only 299 times—fewer than a quarter of the races—and the total payout of $1,937.20 fell far short of

Table 7–1. Performance of Consensus Choices
in Horse Races

Choice	Number chosen	Number finishing:		
		First	Second	Third
First	1,207	299	204	134
Second	1,152	177	189	168
Third	860	119	116	108
Total	3,219	595	509	410

[table continued on next page]

the $2,414 required to bet $2 on each of the 1,207 selections. None of the other choices fared much better.

The reason for this result should be obvious. You can't win by betting on the horses that everybody else is betting on. Your object is not to pick winners, but to maximize your expectation. To do this, you must look for unpopular winners, which may win less often but pay more when they do win.

General Expectations

One way to do this is to look for trends in the public's betting and then go against the track. We see one trend in table 7-1; the $5,434 returned on show bets is significantly greater than the $5,120 paid on win bets. Other figures show the same trend. But before you get excited about this, notice that you'd have to bet $6,438 [$2 on each of the 3,219 selections] to get that $5,434 return. This means that bettors who simply bet on consensus choices to show are still fighting a house percentage of over 15%.

The slight advantage for show bets over win bets on these horses must be balanced by a *dis*advantage for show bets on other horses. When all horses are considered, show bets must pay off less than win bets, because breakage gobbles up a bigger percentage of the smaller show payoffs. On the show bets tabulated in table 7-1, breakage averaged 3%, but it was only 1% on the win payoffs. Nevertheless, in this tabulation, the show bettors came out ahead of the win bettors. This is because betting on favorites to show is not very exciting, and those who do it have less company in their pool.

Table 7-1. continued

| Total payoff on $2 bets and percentage loss | | |
Win	Place	Show
$1,937 [19.8]	$1,953 [19.1]	$1,987 [17.7]
$1,744 [24.3]	$1,856 [19.4]	$1,977 [14.2]
$1,439 [16.3]	$1,433 [16.7]	$1,470 [14.5]
$5,120 [20.5]	$5,242 [18.6]	$5,434 [15.6]

At the other end of the scale, we might therefore expect people who back long shots to do better by betting on win rather than show. A tabulation of results of another 2,000 races confirms this. Defining a long shot as a horse that pays $8 or more to show, I found that show bets on these horses paid a total of $8,239, whereas win bets on the same horses paid a total of $9,828 [even though wins were only one-fourth as frequent as the show payoffs].

Apparently show bettors on long shots have far too much company, and they get a very poor return, in general. However, it does not follow that you will get a good return by betting long shots to win; it's just better than betting them to show.

Specific Expectations

The general statistics quoted above are virtually useless for purposes of figuring your expectation on a specific bet [although they can guide you in improving your expectation if you have nothing else to go on]. To compute your expectation, you need to know the true odds on your horse as well as the betting odds. Ideally, you would like to find an *overlay*—a horse on which the betting odds are greater than the true odds, making your expected return bigger than your bet. But the true odds are hard even to define in a horse race, no matter how good a handicapper you are.

However, there is a way to compare certain bets and determine that one bet has a greater expectation than another. [That's better than nothing, even though you still don't know if either bet gives you a sufficient expectation.] We begin by noticing that, in table 7-1, the second and third consensus

Table 7-2. Tote Board for an Eight-Horse Race

WIN 10000		PLACE 8000		SHOW 10000	
1. 564	5. 2001	1. 441	5. 1607	1. 880	5. 1620
2. 1776	6. 1492	2. 1517	6. 1215	2. 1733	6. 1302
3. 1066	7. 917	3. 707	7. 570	3. 1111	7. 1206
4. 1984	8. 200	4. 1783	8. 160	4. 1848	8. 300

Numbers at the top show total amounts bet on win, place, and show, respectively. Other numbers show amounts bet on respective horses; these are updated frequently before the race begins.

choices—the "sound" horses—have just about equal probability of finishing first, second, or third. So if you bet on a sound horse, you can expect to collect three times on show bets and twice on place bets for each time you collect on a win bet.

This means that a show bet on a sound horse will give you a greater expectation than a win bet on that same horse if the anticipated show payoff is more than one-third of the anticipated win payoff. You can deduce the anticipated payoffs from the numbers shown on the "tote board," an example of which is given in table 7-2.

An exact calculation of each payoff is not necessary, and for place and show it is not even possible at the moment the race begins, because it depends on which other horses are in the money besides your own. But, for a given horse, the bet with the greatest expectation has to be the one with the least company in the pool. For example, if you like[3] horse number 5 in this table, you see that it has 20% of the win pool, 20% of the place pool, and only 16% of the show pool. That makes a bet on show the outstanding choice, assuming that these percentages hold up until the race begins.[4]

To verify this statement, look at table 7-3 in which the anticipated payoffs for this race are shown. Place and show are calculated on the basis of the "worst case," which occurs when the two top favorites finish in the money with your horse.[5] Horse 5 pays $8.40, $4.00, and $3.20, so show is better than win, which in turn is a shade better than place.

There are times when show bettors do a lot better indeed.

Table 7-3. Expected Payoffs in an Eight-Horse Race
When Bet Totals Are as Shown in Table 7–2

WIN		PLACE		SHOW	
1. 30.00	5. 8.40	1. 12.20	5. 4.00	1. 5.00	5. 3.20
2. 9.40	6. 11.20	2. 4.20	6. 5.00	2. 3.20	6. 3.80
3. 15.80	7. 18.40	3. 8.00	7. 9.80	3. 4.20	7. 4.00
4. 8.40	8. 85.00	4. 3.80	8. 32.20	4. 3.00	8. 12.20

The worst possible case is assumed for both place and show payoffs.

Show bets occasionally pay more than win bets on the same horse! A few summers ago, in the Delaware Oaks at Delaware Park, Gallant Bloom was the winner, paying $3.40, $2.80, and $7.20. The second-place horse, Pit Bunny, returned $7.20 on a place bet and a whopping $19.60 on a show bet. White Xmass paid $26 to show.

These inflated show payoffs were the work of "The Man with the Black Bag," a character who often appeared at various tracks to bet thousands of dollars on one of the favored horses to show. When his horse, Shuvee, finished fourth, the winning show bettors shared a $37,000 show pool, of which $30,000 had been bet on Shuvee.

If Shuvee had finished in the money, the other bettors would not have profited from this huge pool, because the $30,000 would have been set aside for the Shuvee backers. But even the experts' first pick finishes in the money only about half of the time [according to table 7-1]. Therefore any large show pool like the one in the Delaware Oaks must offer a potential windfall to the other show bettors, and people who pay attention to the tote board will be able to take advantage of it. [The bag man will place his bets early, because he wants to attract bets against his horse. He knows, or should know, that by inflating one pool, he makes all the other horses look like better bets in that pool, and this helps raise the odds on his horse.]

If you ever have an irresistible urge to risk a bagful of money on a single bet, don't do it at a racetrack. The more you bet on any one horse, the worse your odds become. For example, suppose you wanted to bet on horse number 5 to win (table 7-2). A $2 bet would return $8.40; that's a profit of $6.40, making the odds 3.2 to 1. A $2,000 bet would drive the odds down to 1.6 to 1 and give you a profit of $3,200 (work this out yourself). And betting $20,000 gives you a potential profit of only $2,000—less profit than you'd make on a $2,000 bet! Betting so much on one horse that you drive down the odds is just betting against yourself.[6]

Parlays

In chapter 3 we saw that you could get a big payoff on a small investment by playing a reverse martingale. In sports betting this is called a parlay. The advantage of this tactic in a casino is that you have the possibility of a big-odds payoff without bucking the huge house edge that goes with the big-odds games. But in racing, because the house percentage is the same on all bets, the parlay loses its appeal. In general, it is better to make one bet at large odds than to parlay two bets at smaller odds, because the track takes two bites out of your parlay. This statement might seem hard to verify in practice; you can't compare a long shot in one race with better horses in two races. But you can prove it for yourself by studying the results of daily-double or similar combination bets.

The daily double is a single bet on the winners of the first two races. You could make the equivalent of a daily-double bet by placing a win bet on the first race and then putting all your winnings (if any) on another win bet in the second race. On any given day, the daily double could pay off either more or less than the parlay, depending on how heavily your horses are backed in the daily double (a separate pool, of course) and in the individual races. But on the average, because the track gets only one bite out of the daily-double bet, the daily double pays about 25% more than the parlay would.

You don't have to take my word for this. You can check it out by following the race results in the newspapers. The same reasoning applies to all other combination bets.

Please don't conclude from this discussion that the daily double will make you rich. There is still the house percentage of more than 15%. You should always expect to lose at the races, but the possibility of a big payoff at least provides some excitement for your money.

Bookmakers

If you can't get to a racetrack, you may be tempted to place a bet with a bookie. Aside from the illegality of it, there are strong reasons to resist this temptation. The bookie normally pays off at the same odds as the track, which means that you should expect to lose at the usual rate of about 17%. And you can't watch the tote board to try to pick up a last-minute bargain. Maybe you are a good enough judge of horses to pick winners, but keep in mind that the real problem is to pick overlays. If you are so good at judging horses and horse-players that you can pick unpopular winners, then you have been wasting your time reading this chapter.

Away from the track, the best way to win is—you guessed it—*to be* the bookie. If you, as the bookie, pay off at the track odds, then you will make the same rate of profit as the track as long as your customers bet on each horse in the same proportion as the bettors at the track. For example, suppose the bettors at the track support Bumfuzzle with bets totaling $4,000 out of a total of $12,000 in win bets. If Bumfuzzle wins, the track will pay $5 on each $2 bet, for a total payout of $10,000 and a profit of $2,000. If you, the bookie, also have one-third of your total "action" on Bumfuzzle, you stand to pocket $1 out of every $6 bet, just as the track does. But if all your bets are on Bumfuzzle, you could be very nervous; a Bumfuzzle victory will put you in a large hole.

Of course, if Bumfuzzle loses, a bookie with all of his action on Bumfuzzle will make 100% profit. But bookies are not gamblers. They avoid gambling by "laying off" bets on other bookies. If bookie A gets so much action on Bumfuzzle that he could lose money on it, he "lays off" some of it by betting on Bumfuzzle himself with bookie B. If B also has too much on that steed, he lays some off with a bigger bookie, C. Eventually the money could find its way to a bookie who has a confederate at the track, who places bets on Bumfuzzle there.

This chain of events simultaneously lays off the bets and cuts down the odds that the bookies would have to pay on the remaining bets that they hold on Bumfuzzle. Here we have a perfect example of a free market at work, setting prices by the action of supply and demand.

But what if the bets come in too late for the bookies to lay them off? [This is what happened in the scam described in note 6.] The bookie, if he is cautious, will simply refuse to take those bets. He might remember that scam.

CHAPTER 8

Sporting Chances

Sports are a big business, and one thing that makes them big is the uncertainty. There are dramatic changes in players' performances and in performances of whole teams, resulting from unpredictable causes. This generates excitement and also betting.

Betting on sports is the domain of the compulsive gambler. It gives him a chance to bet every day, simply by making a phone call, and then to watch on TV as his chances rise and fall during each game. It also gives him a chance to be a huge loser. The house percentage on sports betting runs from good to phenomenal—for the bookie.

But you can enjoy sports, without betting, as a participant, a spectator, or a second-guesser. For you second-guessers, this chapter will present probabilities relating to some of the "book" strategies in sports.

Sports Betting

Long-Odds Bets

In sports betting, as in other forms of organized gambling, the long-odds propositions are the worst. For example, if you bet on which teams will win the pennant races in baseball, or the seventy-six-team playoffs in other sports, you can get very high odds on many teams. Table 8-1 shows baseball odds at the start of one season.

Even though we do not know the true odds on any given team, it is not hard to compute the house percentage on such

"They must expect him to bunt."

Drawing by R. J. D. Copyright © 1936, 1964 by The New Yorker Magazine, Inc.

Table 8-1. Preseason Odds on
Baseball Pennant Winners, 1978

Team	Odds	Bet needed to return $1,000	Team	Odds	Bet needed to return $1,000
New York	5–7	$583.33			
Kansas City	7–2	222.22	Cincinnati	7–5	$416.67
Texas	7–2	222.22	Los Angeles	7–5	416.67
Boston	4–1	200.00	Philadelphia	2–1	333.33
California	6–1	142.86	Pittsburgh	6–1	142.86
Baltimore	15–1	62.50	St. Louis	12–1	76.92
Chicago	60–1	16.39	San Francisco	20–1	47.62
Detroit	75–1	13.16	Houston	30–1	32.26
Minnesota	75–1	13.16	San Diego	75–1	13.16
Milwaukee	100–1	9.90	Chicago	100–1	9.90
Cleveland	300–1	3.32	Montreal	100–1	9.90
Oakland	300–1	3.32	New York	200–1	4.98
Seattle	1,000–1	1.00	Atlanta	300–1	3.32
Toronto	1,000–1	1.00		Total	$1,507.59
	Total	$1,494.38			

bets. We simply figure how much you would have to bet on
each team to get a return of $1,000. These amounts, shown
in the table, add up to about $1,500. So the odds-makers
who assigned these odds have provided the bookmakers with
a profit of $500 on each $1,500 bet, as long as the bets on
each team are in the proportions shown in the table. That's a
house edge of about 33%, and the same edge holds true for
playoff bets in other sports. The bookies don't have to know
a thing about the chances of each team. As long as they get
enough action on each team to keep the bets in proportion,
they are guaranteed their 33% profit.

If the trend of the betting causes these proportions to
change, then the odds are adjusted accordingly. For example,
if crazy Clevelanders back the Indians enough to make the
total bet on the "Tribe" reach $10 out of every $1,500 bet,
then the odds against Cleveland would be changed to 100 to
1 (matching the odds paid on Milwaukee). If the bets on
Cleveland were made mostly in the Cleveland area, bookies
there would probably lay off some of them with bookies in

other cities to keep the relative amounts bet on different teams in line with the national averages.

You baseball fans have a daily opportunity to bet on another poor proposition. You can pick three players, and if your players get a total of six hits or more that day, you win. Good luck! The true odds on this bet can be approximated fairly well. Assume [optimistically] that your three players have a collective batting average of .333. You might expect them to total twelve times at bat on a day when all three are healthy. [Only one game counts in a double-header.] The probability of six or more hits is then the sum

$$924 \times (1/3)^6 \times (2/3)^6 + 792 \times (1/3)^7 \times (2/3)^5 \ldots + (1/3)^{12}$$

which equals about 1/6. [This is the sum of the binomial probabilities of six, seven, eight, nine, ten, eleven, and twelve successes in twelve trials; see chapter 2.] So if your bookie pays 3 to 1 odds, he will return $4 on one of six $1 bets, keeping the $5 from the other five bets, and make a profit of $1 to $6 in bets—a healthy 16% edge, even though you had magnificent hitters going for you.

Bets on Single Games

The smallest house edge for the bookie is provided by bets on individual games. In many cases, instead of adjusting the odds, the bookmakers adjust the chance of success by "spotting" points to one team or the other. For example, Grambling may be a 32-point favorite over Slippery Rock in college football; in that case, a bet on Slippery Rock wins even if Slippery Rock loses, as long as the loss is by fewer than 32 points. If Grambling wins by exactly 32, the bet is called off.

The purpose of the spot, or "spread," is to make the betting public, collectively, think that each side has an equal chance so that half of the bets come in on each side. If the 32-point spread causes too much money to pour in on Slippery Rock, then the spot will be reduced to make those bets less attractive and bring in more money on Grambling.

Once the spread is properly adjusted to equalize the betting on each side, the bookie has a sure thing. He makes his profit by demanding 11 to 10 odds from the bettor, no matter which side he takes. This gives the bookie an edge of 4.54%; each time he takes in $22 ($11 on each side), he gives back $21 to the winner and keeps $1.

In games such as hockey, where few goals are scored, a 1-point spot is common. But such a spot is not as good as it looks, because overtime eliminates most ties, preventing you from winning on those results. Even though you have a "spot," your team must win the game if you are to win your bet.

In baseball, spots are not given (unless a game looks very one-sided). Instead, the odds depend on which side the bettor wants to take. If the game is even (a "pick"), the bettor on either side must give the usual 11 to 10 odds. But the odds are strongly dependent upon the pitchers. If Valenzuela is pitching, the odds might be quoted as 6–7. This abbreviation means that you win $6 on a successful $10 bet on Valenzuela's team, and you must bet only $7 to win $10 if you are betting against his team. The bookie's percentage averages about 4% (3.54% in this example).

Parlays

Bookies will also allow you to parlay two bets simultaneously, giving you odds of 2.4 to 1 on two even propositions (on each of which you would normally give the bookie 11 to 10 odds). Your chance of collecting is 1/4, which means the true odds are 3 to 1 against you, assuming no ties. (If a tie occurs, it may be agreed that the second proposition is handled as a single bet.) On four $10 bets, the bookie pays out $34 once and keeps a $6 profit, or 15%.

You can do worse. There are football cards that permit you to select (giving or taking a spot) up to ten teams. If you select three teams, you collect at 5 to 1 when all are right— and you lose if there are any ties. Even if ties were impossible, you would be fighting an edge of 25% on that one (you average one $60 return on eight $10 bets). And if you try to pick ten winners, your payoff is 100 to 1—but the true odds are 1,023 to 1, even without ties. They also offer you a small payoff if nine of your ten are right, but that still makes it a far worse proposition than the numbers game.

Touts

If you had time to study the teams carefully, it should not be hard to overcome the 4% to 5% edge on single games. You are not betting against the bookies, remember; you are betting against the "line," which is set by the bettors themselves. If you consistently know more than they do, it is possible for you to win consistently.

If you don't have time to do the homework, there are friendly people out there who will study the teams and advise you—for a price (up to $500 per month, according to advertising received here). Some of these advisory services claim to be 80% or 90% correct against the point "spread." And they list their successes to prove it. If you doubt their word, they offer the clinching argument: Buy a few special selections at $35 to $50 apiece, and you won't have to pay for any that are wrong. (But they won't cover the losses of your bets.) Here are two more big ifs:

1. If they are telling the truth about their successes, they still might not be telling the *whole* truth. These services offer numerous categories of "membership," and they give different selections to each one. There are bound to be some categories that are more fortunate than others. Which ones do you think they report on in their advertising? (A four-week trial subscription to one service produced twelve winners and ten losers. But the service continued to report much higher winning percentages on their other subscriptions.)

2. If all of their selections are strong favorites to beat the spread, the selections might not be such favorites if the point spread changes. When they report 77% correct against the "line," they refer to the line that was quoted *before their selections became known*. If the service is really good (and expensive), people will immediately bet enough on their choices to change the point spread considerably—in a few minutes. Who knows how good your chances are if you make your bet too late and have to spot 7 more points?

One service became famous for its "lock of the year," which was correct for ten straight years. Their pick for the eleventh year was a team that the "line" favored by 4 points. When the "lock" selection became known, that team became a 12-point favorite. A friend of mine who is a regular sports bettor has done well recently by waiting for this "lock" to come out and change the point spread, then betting against the lock. He collected when that 12-point favorite didn't even win the game.

The touts are aware of the problem of the shifting spread. One ad says, "Can you keep a secret for four hours?" And they proceed to explain how you can "kill Vegas" if you don't spill the secret. But Vegas, whoever he is, could subscribe to their service and find out the "secret" for himself, if he needed to. One service sent me a letter that read, "Your name came up because you and I go back a long way." [I had been on the mailing list for eight months.] "You are a person I am proud to call friend and customer." [I don't know him and never paid him a nickel.] "Because of that, I'm inviting you to join my exclusive . . ." If they'll take me, they'll take anybody [as long as he comes up with the $1,000].

The touts also emphasize making their selections at the last minute. Some of their services give only one or two weekly choices, real "locks," which are allegedly not settled upon until the day of the game. These are supposedly those rare games for which the players' conditions and the spread make it an exceptionally high probability that the choice will be a winner. That sounds reasonable until you read on and find out that two basketball games to be played in April, a month after the ad appears, are going to be "lock" selections no matter what the point spread is!

Sports Probabilities and Strategy

Baseball and American football are unusual among team sports because of the break that occurs before each play. This permits the coach or manager to dictate strategy during the game to a greater degree than in other sports. It also makes it easier to analyze individual plays and performance and to compile statistics.

Perhaps the relative dearth of statistics is one reason why soccer has not caught on in America. In a baseball game, even if the score is 1–0, at least eighteen players have all kinds of individual statistics. You'll be impressed by the fact that Henderson stole two bases, even if he didn't score a run.

To make soccer more popular in America, all somebody has to do is invent a reliable way to compile a variety of individual and team statistics—say, "pass interceptions," "blocked shots," or "time of possession." Every now and then they could stop the game to say something like, "That was the five-hundredth blocked shot of Beckenbauer's career," and present him with the ball.

Baseball

Of all sports, baseball lends itself best to mathematical analysis, because so many individual statistics are kept on the players, and the same situations recur repeatedly. In addition to the statistics, there is a rich treasury of folklore to guide managers in making decisions. Following this folklore is called "going by the book."

The people who wrote this "book" knew nothing about probabilities, but it doesn't matter, for all managers go by the same book. Each team has a statistician who does know the probabilities, but if his advice runs counter to the book, nobody believes him.

If you follow baseball at all, you may enjoy some occasional "grandstand managing." Of course, the manager, with his vast experience, knows more about the game and the players than we do; but often what hurts us is what we "know" that isn't so! Let's see if we can find some things that every manager knows that aren't so.

1. The sacrifice bunt is often used to advance a runner one base when nobody is out, especially in the late innings. If it were used only when the batter is an elderly pitcher or the equivalent, there would be no question about the choice.

The use of the strategy in other situations is based on the

belief that, with average hitters due up, [a] a runner on second with one out has a better chance of scoring than a runner on first with nobody out, or [b] a runner on third with one out has a better chance of scoring than a runner on second with nobody out.

According to a study by Earnshaw Cook, who analyzed 20,000 baseball games, the first proposition is barely correct, and the second is dead wrong.[1] Cook gives the probabilities of scoring, with average hitters who do not bunt, as

- Runner on first, 0 out: 43%
- Runner on second, 1 out: 45%
- Runner on first, 1 out: 29%
- Runner on second, 0 out: 60%
- Runner on third, 1 out: 54%

Furthermore, when first is occupied and nobody is out, the bunt is successful only an average of 74% of the time [according to Cook]. When it fails, there is usually a runner on first with one out and a 29% chance of scoring. So ordering an average hitter to bunt actually reduces the probability of scoring even one run, and it clobbers the chance of scoring more than one run.[2] If Cook's figures are correct, the bunt is even worse when a runner is on second with nobody out. And with both first and second occupied and nobody out, the bunt often kills a potentially big inning while giving a respite to a pitcher who has just been tagged for two successive hits.

You may well wonder whether Cook's figures, compiled many years ago, are still valid today. You can check them out for yourself just by recording what happens in those situations. A few dozen games should give you enough statistical accuracy to test the conclusions. My own test gives figures that are remarkably close to Cook's.

2. The stolen base is another way to advance a runner, but if it is successful, it does not give up an out. Since some base stealers are successful over 80% of the time, it is often a winning strategy, and it certainly adds excitement to the game. When a runner is on first base with two out, his average probability of scoring is only 14%. By stealing second, he raises that probability to 26%. So in this "double or nothing" situation, it is profitable to try to steal if the runner has a mere 55% chance of success. With one out, the steal attempt is indicated if the chance of success is 64% or better, and with nobody out, a success probability of 72% or better is needed to make it a winning proposition.

Unfortunately, I must report that stealing a lot of bases has a very small effect on a team's success in the long run. This is because the better running teams total only about one hundred fifty steals a season—fewer than one per game—and we can see from the above percentages that a steal gains only about an eighth of a run, on the average. The very best base-stealing teams steal about fifty more bases than their average opposition, thereby gaining about six runs, which might translate into two or three additional victories at best.

This conclusion is supported by statistics on overall performance of the teams that lead their divisions in base stealing. As reported by Bill James, the average final standing of teams that lead in base stealing is lower than that of teams that lead in any other offensive category [for example, batting average, home runs, slugging average].[3] This should be no surprise; the teams that lead in these categories have an edge of many more than fifty extra bases on their average opposition.

This result underscores our comments about the sacrifice bunt. If good base stealing, which usually gains a base without giving up an out, is so unproductive, it is clear that giving up an out to advance a runner one base has very little going for it.

3. The intentional base on balls is often given to avoid a dangerous hitter and pitch to one who might be more friendly. But it is also awarded to average hitters to set up a double-play situation when a runner is on third with fewer than two outs. Except near the end of the game, when one run can be decisive, this is a dubious strategy. The double-play possibility cuts down, by about 9%, the chance that one run will score. But putting another man on base increases, by about

18%, the chance that two runs will score. That second run might be the deciding run, rather than the first one.

4. Platooning is the answer to statistics showing that left-handed batters do better against right-handed pitchers than they do against left handers, and that the converse is true for right-handed batters. So when you face a left-handed pitcher, you load your lineup with right-handed batters. Later in the game, when a right-handed pitcher comes in, you bring in your left-handed batters (and hope you can win the game before another left hander comes in to pitch).

True, some good left-handed batters are noticeably inept against left-handed pitchers. Statistics on 35,000 times at bat by 130 batters in both leagues show that the overall average for left handers is about .030 lower against left-handed pitching than against right-handed pitching. For right-handed batters the difference is only half as great.[4] But you seldom have players who are so interchangeable that this overall difference—about one hit in 50 times at bat—is crucial. Many other considerations should outweigh ''handedness.''

One consideration is illustrated by the 1972 National League championship playoff. Pittsburgh led Cincinnati, 3 to 2, going into the ninth inning of the final game. Pittsburgh's pitcher, Ramon Hernandez, had retired the two men he faced in the eighth, striking out one of them. Hernandez had had an excellent season as a relief pitcher, with five wins, no losses, fourteen saves, and a 1.67 earned-run average. He had given up only one hit in three and one-third playoff innings.

But he was left handed, and the first three batters for Cincinnati in the ninth were right handed. So in came right-handed Dave Giusti to pitch, and out went the baseball as the first batter, Johnny Bench, hit a home run. The other two right-handed batters also hit safely, and Cincinnati won, 4 to 3.

Giusti got the goat horns, but the real goat was the Pittsburgh manager. Giusti also had pitched well that season; if neither pitcher had been in the game already, it might have made sense to go for that 2% edge. But athletes aren't machines; they have good days and bad days, for unpredictable reasons. If your pitcher has been performing well, as Hernandez had, there had to be more than a 2% chance that any replacement would be worse. Anyone who has an off day less than 2% of the time has to be a superperson.

Football

One peculiarity of American football is that the probability of scoring in the last two minutes of either half is far greater than during any other two-minute time interval. That this is so is partly because the clock is stopped more often during those two minutes, but it is also a result of a strange maneuver. After stopping their opponents' offense for twenty-eight minutes, a team often changes to a "prevent" defense that allows the opponents to score in one minute![5]

The purpose of this spread-out defense is to "prevent" a long touchdown pass—a play that must have considerably less than a 10% chance of success.[6] The result is that a team that was going nowhere is suddenly given room to complete several ten- to fifteen-yard passes, get a big psychological lift, and often score quickly. [It takes very little time for a pro team to line up after a pass completion and throw the ball out of bounds to stop the clock.] Contrast this with the strategy in other sports, in which a winning method is never changed.

Probabilities on specific plays in football are much harder to assess than those in baseball. This is because the variety of field positions is so much greater, and statistics depend more on the team than the individual. The field-goal attempt is one exception; the range and accuracy of each kicker are well documented, and the defensive team seldom is able to affect the result. Nevertheless, there are other factors that make even these figures difficult to apply when a decision has to be made.

The Cleveland Browns' coach was faced with a difficult decision on a field-goal attempt in a 1981 playoff game against Oakland. Cleveland, down 14–12, had a second down on the Oakland thirteen-yard line with forty-nine seconds to go. A field goal, normally a 75% to 80% chance at that range, would almost surely win the game. But a strong crosswind and the frozen turf had been hard on the kicking game that day. The usually reliable Cleveland kicker had missed an extra point, and he had made only two of four field-goal attempts from that range during the game. There was time to run another play before trying the field goal. What would you do?

Coach Sam Rutigliano opted for a pass into the end zone, and he was roasted mercilessly after it was intercepted to give Oakland the victory. But the choice was not bad, given that the probability of making the field goal appeared to be less than 60%. Let's try to assess the probabilities for the actual decision.

An incomplete pass would preserve the field goal opportunity, hence we can disregard that possibility in computing the probabilities.[7] It is not too optimistic to assume from past experience that a completed pass would be twice as likely as an interception. That would give the Browns 2/3 of the decisions on the pass play, plus the probability, say 60%, of making the field goal when the pass was incomplete. That adds up to more than the straight 60% chance on the immediate field goal attempt.

In general, in such a situation, the pass has to be better than the immediate kick as long as the ratio of completions to interceptions is better than the odds favoring the kick. If you doubt this, put in some actual numbers and work out the compound probabilities for each case.

Conclusions

Sports, especially baseball, present curious contradictions in the use of statistics. Some statistics, such as the left-handed vs. right-handed figures, are overemphasized at the expense of more important factors. Other statistics, such as the dismal success rate for the sacrifice bunt, are ignored.

CHAPTER 9

Contract Bridge

Bridge is an easy game. There is no house percentage to beat, and you can choose the bid or play that gives you the best of the odds. Your opponents can do that too, but these are the same people who give a big edge away to lotteries, racetracks, casinos, and bookies. Why shouldn't they be generous to you, too?

Bridge writers sometimes give the impression that "playing the percentages" in bridge is a complicated business requiring memorization of a lot of tables. But many percentage plays require nothing more than the ability to count up to thirteen. We'll examine some of these plays, and then we'll see how percentages figure in the bidding as well (without requiring knowledge of any particular bidding system).

Probabilities in the Play

Bridge probabilities are simpler than those in blackjack. In bridge you can work out the odds on many plays right at the table, without resorting to a computer. You can see two of the four hands, and your most common problem is simply to determine whether a specific unseen card, say the queen of spades, is on your left or on your right.

Some Propositions

Before looking at any specific hands, let's set up some artificial propositions that have great relevance to probabilities in the play of a hand. Let's begin by assuming that you have no information on the queen of spades, and therefore

107

the probability that it is on your left hand is obviously 1/2. [In practice this is never strictly the case, because you see the opening lead before you see the dummy, but there is no need to concern ourselves with that now.] Then:

Proposition 1. If you could peel back one card at random from the hand of your left-hand opponent [LHO] and look at it, the probability would change. If that card were the queen of spades, then the probability would become 1. If it were not the queen of spades, then the probability would become 12/25, because LHO would have only twelve of the twenty-five randomly selected unseen cards.

Proposition 2. If LHO selected a card to show you—if he were ordered to show you a card but not to show you a face card—then the card that he showed you would have no bearing whatsoever on the probability of his holding the spade queen. The probability would remain 1/2, even though he would have only twelve unseen cards, because those unseen cards would no longer be randomly selected. The probability changes only when you acquire relevant new information; when you know in advance that the card you will see will not be the queen of spades, then seeing that card gives you no information about the location of that queen.

Proposition 3. If LHO were ordered to let you peek at a randomly selected card that was not a spade, your seeing that specific card would not affect the probabilities either. But you could learn a lot from seeing how many non-spades he has to offer you. If he had eleven non-spades, and you could see eight spades in your own two hands, you would know that LHO had been dealt two of the five unseen spades. On two out of five deals when this happens, LHO will have the spade queen, so the probability would become 2/5.

Proposition 4. We can carry Proposition 3 further. If you could look at one of LHO's two spades, chosen at random, and you found that it was not the queen, then LHO would have only one of four randomly selected unseen spades. The probability that he held the queen would then drop to 1/4.

Proposition 5. A different continuation of Proposition 3. Suppose LHO were forced to show you one of his two spades, but was ordered not to show you the queen. Under these conditions, seeing this card would give you no new relevant information. The probability would remain 2/5 as in Proposition 3, not 1/4 as in Proposition 4, because his one unseen spade would not have been randomly selected.

Application

These propositions are quite relevant to actual hands. For example, you are playing seven no trump on the following[1]:

	Spades	*Hearts*	*Diamonds*	*Clubs*
Dummy:	A x x	A x x	A x x x	A J 10
Declarer:	K Q x	K Q x	K Q J x	K x x

Your only possible loser is the third club. You win the first ten tricks in the other three suits, and you notice that LHO followed suit to only two hearts and two spades, whereas RHO had only one diamond. So you know that RHO was dealt five spades, five hearts, one diamond, and therefore only two of the opponents' seven clubs. The odds are thus 5 to 2 that LHO was dealt the queen of clubs [Proposition 3].

It is true that LHO has only three clubs left after ten cards have been played, but the odds are still 5 to 2. Just as in Proposition 5, LHO would never part with the queen, so his two club discards do not change the odds. You confidently play for LHO to hold the queen, knowing that you can ably defend yourself against your partner's wrath if your play fails.

"Book" Probabilities on Suit Breaks

It is not often possible to determine how a suit will divide by counting out all the other suits, as we did on the above hand. At the other extreme, you sometimes want to know the probabilities of various divisions of a suit before you know anything about the distribution of any suit. These probabilities, worked out long ago, appear in many bridge books. The most important ones are shown in table 9-1.

This table should not be considered the last word on suit-break probabilities—it is just the first word. Those probabilities can change drastically when you find out how the other suits are divided. For example, if there are six clubs out and you know that LHO was dealt eight spades, then the probability that LHO holds all six clubs is nil, and the probability that he holds five clubs is minuscule.

If you know how the probabilities in table 9-1 are worked out, you will be better able to see how they change when new information is obtained, and you will also be better able to remember the more important numbers. Let's start with the easier ones and work out a few.

Two cards missing. Say the missing cards are the ace and king of clubs. If a given opponent has the ace, he is entitled to only twelve of the remaining twenty-five cards; therefore the probability that this same opponent has the king (or any other specific card) is 12/25. Thus the probability that the opponents' clubs will divide 2–0, with the two cards being in either hand, is 12/25, or 48%, as given in the fifth column of table 9-1. The probability that a specific hand holds both clubs is half of this, 6/25, or 24%. (Probabilities that specific cards are in specific hands are given in the fourth column of table 9-1.)

Three cards missing. To get all three cards, a given opponent must first get two of them, which is a 24% chance. He then gets eleven of the other twenty-four cards, so his chance of getting the third club (say the queen) is 11/24 when he already has the ace and king. His combined probability of getting the ace, king, and queen is thus (11/24) × 24%, or 11%. The other opponent also has an 11% chance of getting all three clubs, leaving a 78% chance that one opponent gets two and the other opponent gets one club, as shown in the sixth column of table 9-1.

Four cards missing. The chance that all four are on your left is equal to the 11% probability that the first three are on your left, multiplied by 10/23, because your LHO gets ten of the other twenty-three cards. That comes to 11/230; the chance that either opponent has all four is twice this, or 11/115.

The chance that a specific set of three cards out of four is on your left is equal to the same 11% probability that the first three are on your left, multiplied by the probability of 13/23 that the fourth card is on your right. The result is a probability of 143/2,300 for a *specific* 3–1 break. The number of such breaks, as shown in the third column of table 9-1, is eight. This is because there are four possible singletons, and the singleton can be in either hand. So the total probability of all 3–1 breaks is 8 × [143/2,300], or 286/575 [column five]. In general, the number in column five is the product of the number in column three and the number in column four.

The probability of a 2–2 break is what is left, 234/575. The probability of a specific 2–2 break is 1/6 of this, or 39/575, because [as indicated in column three of the table] there are six possible pairs that a given opponent can have out of four cards.

Notice from these numbers that a specific 2–2 break is exactly 12/11 as likely as a specific 3–1 break: 39/575 = [12/11] × 143/2,300. We can see the reason for this important ratio by starting with a specific 2–1 break and adding one card. The player with the singleton has twelve chances to get that other card, while the player who already has two cards in the suit has only eleven chances to make it three. In the same way, we can see why a specific 3–3 break is 11/10 as likely as a specific 4–2 break. [Again see column four of table 9-1.]

Using the Book Probabilities to Play a Hand

It is not necessary to memorize table 9-1 in order to play bridge, but if you want to win, you should learn the important numbers. For example, you should learn that four, six, or eight cards are unlikely to be divided equally. Then when you have to play a hand like the following one, you will know what to do.

Table 9-1. Suit Division Probabilities: Bridge and Pinochle

Number of cards held by opponents	Division between opponents	Number of ways to make this division	Probability of each way, exact fraction, bridge	Total probability of this division		
				Exact fraction, bridge	Percentage, bridge	Percentage, pinochle
2	1-1	2	13/50	13/25	52.0	51.7
	2-0	2	6/25	12/25	48.0	48.3
3	2-1	6	13/100	39/50	78.0	77.6
	3-0	2	11/100	11/50	22.0	22.4
4	2-2	6	39/575	234/575	40.7	40.2
	3-1	8	143/2,300	286/575	49.7	49.8
	4-0	2	11/230	11/115	9.6	10.0
5	3-2	20	39/1,150	78/115	67.8	67.1
	4-1	10	13/460	13/46	28.3	28.7
	5-0	2	9/460	9/230	3.9	4.2

Table 9-1. continued

Number of cards held by opponents	Division between opponents	Number of ways to make this division	Probability of each way, exact fraction, bridge	Total probability of this division		
				Exact fraction, bridge	Percentage, bridge	Percentage, pinochle
6	3-3	20	143/8,050	286/805	35.5	34.8
	4-2	30	13/805	78/161	48.5	48.3
	5-1	12	39/3,220	117/805	14.5	15.2
	6-0	2	6/805	12/805	1.5	1.7
7	4-3	70	143/16,100	143/230	62.2	61.0
	5-2	42	117/16,100	351/1,150	30.5	31.0
	6-1	14	39/8,050	39/575	6.8	7.4
	7-0	2	3/1,150	3/575	0.5	0.6
8	4-4	70	143/30,590	1,001/3,059	32.7	31.8
	5-3	112	1,287/305,900	36,036/76,475	47.1	46.7
	6-2	56	234/76,475	13,104/76,475	17.1	18.0
	7-1	16	39/21,850	312/10,925	2.9	3.3
	8-0	2	9/10,925	18/10,925	0.2	0.2

	Spades	Hearts	Diamonds	Clubs
Dummy:	x x x	Q x x x x	A Q J	x x
Declarer:	A K x x	A K	x x x x x	A x

Playing 3 no trump, you get a club lead, so you must take nine tricks without losing the lead; there is no time to fish for information. You have seven top tricks; you can get the other two if the hearts are divided 3–3, or if LHO has the diamond king. But if both opponents follow to two rounds of hearts, you can't find out whether they are 4–2 or 3–3 without leading a diamond. The 4–2 break is considerably more likely than a 3–3 break, so you must try the diamond finesse, a 50% chance, and pass up the heart possibility.

Using the Book Probabilities to Play a Suit

Table 9-2 shows some commonly encountered holdings in a single suit, which present a close choice between two different plays. Let's see the reason for choosing one play over the other.

In a, you are missing only two cards. If you lead from the South hand and West plays low, East is a 13 to 12 favorite to have the king, so the ace is the proper play.

In b, you have a similar choice of finessing for the queen. You play the ace, then lead a small one. If West follows with the last low card, you have a choice of playing for the opponents' holdings to be either

	x x	opposite	Q x
or	Q x x	opposite	x

Since a *specific* 2–2 break is 12/11 as likely as a specific 3–1 break, you should play the king, hoping for holding 1.

In c, you have the same sort of choice on the third round of the suit, after opponents have played all the small cards. Their holdings were either

	x x x	opposite	J x x
or	J x x x	opposite	x x

Table 9-2. Recommended Plays and Reasonable Alternatives

	North-South's clubs	Recommended play	Alternative, and odds against its success	To make alternative the favorite, East must be dealt, in known suits
a.	A Q J x x x x x x x x	Play ace	Finesse queen; 13 to 12.	Two more cards than West
b.	K J 10 x A x x x x	Play ace and king	Finesse on second round; 12 to 11.	Two more cards than West
c.	Q 10 x x A K x	Play ace, king, and queen	Play ace and king, then finesse ten; 11 to 10.	Two more cards than West
d.	J 9 x x K Q x	Lead toward king; if West takes king or queen with ace, play jack on third round	Start as in recommended play, but finesse nine on third round; 11 to 10.	Two more cards than West
e.	K J 9 x A x x x	Play ace, then finesse jack	Play ace, then finesse nine; 6 to 5.	Three more cards than West
f.	K J 9 x x x x x x	Finesse jack	Finesse nine; 13 to 11.	Three more cards than West
g.	A Q 10 x x x x x x x	Finesse queen	Finesse ten; 13 to 11.	Three more cards than West

Again, you should play for the even split. A specific 3-3 break is an 11 to 10 favorite over a specific 4-2 break.

The same reasoning applies to d, where you must choose between playing for

	A x x	opposite	10 x x
or	A 10 x x	opposite	x x

assuming that West has topped your king or queen with the ace. The even split is again an 11 to 10 favorite.

Combination e is yet another variation on the same theme. After South wins the ace and leads a spot card, and West follows with the last low card, only the queen and ten remain out. South could play the nine, hoping that the opponents hold

Q 10 x x   opposite   x

or he could play the jack, hoping that they hold

Q x x   opposite   10 x

The latter is a more likely holding. A specific 3-2 break is favored over a specific 4-1 break by 12 to 10, for reasons that you should be able to work out for yourself by now.

You can work out the rest of the odds in the third column yourself. The fourth column shows what you might do if you have information on the count of another suit. I'll discuss that below.

The Principle of Restricted Choice

The discussion of combination e omitted a third possible holding:

10 x x   opposite   Q x

If this is the opponents' holding, you win by hopping up with the king and felling the queen on the second round. This play would seem to be equal to the play of the jack, because East is just as likely to be dealt the queen-x as the ten-x.

But we know something else; we know that West has not played the ten! If West had been dealt ten-x-x, he would have no reason not to play the ten on the second trick. This is like Proposition 4; because the cards we have seen from West did not include the ten, the probability that he holds the ten is smaller than it was originally. On the other hand, if West had held queen-x-x, he would never have played the queen on the first or second trick. Therefore the probability that he holds the queen is not diminished after you see his two spot cards.

The governing principle here is called ''The Principle of Restricted Choice.'' The general statement of this principle is:

If there are two possible holdings from which an opponent could have played a certain card or cards, the more likely holding is the one that gave him no choice of plays.

Holding ten-x-x, West had a choice of plays. He might have chosen to play the ten. Holding queen-x-x, he had no choice; he would always play small cards to the first two tricks, because playing the queen would give up all chance of winning a trick. So, at this point, queen-x-x is the more likely holding for West to have had.

The classic application of the principle of restricted choice is on the following combination (call it the club suit):

West: A 10 x x x   East: K x x x

East, the declarer, plays the club king, and North follows with the jack. On the next lead from East, South plays the last low club. Only one club remains, the queen. Who has it? North was dealt either queen-jack doubleton or jack singleton. According to the principle of restricted choice, the singleton is more likely, because that is the holding that gave him no choice of plays. Let's verify this with some numbers.

We have seen that a specific 2–2 break occurs 12/11 as often as a specific 3–1 break, so North is dealt queen-jack doubleton twelve times for each eleven times he is dealt the singleton jack. The singleton queen occurs as often as the singleton jack, so thirty-four deals on which North has one of these holdings will divide, on the average,

> Twelve deals: queen-jack doubleton
> Eleven deals: jack singleton
> Eleven deals: queen singleton

If you always assumed that North held a singleton when he played an honor on the first round, you would be right twenty-two times out of thirty-four—not a bad percentage.

Some players argue that the eleven deals on which the queen is singleton are irrelevant here, because North is known to have played the jack. North is dealt the jack on only eleven of the twenty-three relevant deals, so the holding of the singleton jack must be an 11-to-12 underdog. The same argument can be used when North's first play is the queen. But something must be wrong, because if you act on this reasoning on all thirty-four deals, you will succeed only twelve times instead of twenty-two.

The fallacy lies in changing the verb, in mid-argument, from "played" [the jack] to being "dealt" [the jack]. North's best policy with Q J is to play one or the other at random. So he will play the jack on only seventeen of those twenty-three "relevant" deals—six times when he has the Q J and eleven times when he has the jack. The resulting odds are 11 to 6 that, when he plays the jack, he does not have the queen. The reasoning here is much like that in Proposition 4; when the randomly selected card is not the queen, the probability that the player was dealt the queen is reduced.

Can East do better by not playing randomly—perhaps by always playing the queen when he holds queen-jack? No. As his opponent you will still win on twenty-two of the thirty-four deals, because your play does not depend on what he plays. And if you do begin to notice what he is doing, you can only do better. You will know to finesse only when he plays the jack, and you will succeed on twenty-three deals of

Table 9-3. Restricted-Choice Plays

North–South hold:	Play	Odds favoring play
a. K 10 x x x A x x x	Ace. If East drops an honor, finesse tenspot next.	11 to 6
b. Q 9 x x A K x	Ace and king. If East drops an honor, finesse ninespot.	20 to 11
c. K J 8 x A x x x	Ace. If East plays the nine or ten, finesse the eightspot.	5 to 3
d. A J 10 x x x x x x	Jack (finesse). If this loses, then finesse the tenspot.	11 to 6
e. Q 8 x x A K x	Ace and king. If East's two plays are jack-ten, jack-nine, or ten-nine, finesse the eightspot.	5 to 2

the thirty-four. It doesn't pay to be predictable in a card game.

A Pittsburgher named Leo Schmertz once held this combination as his club suit in a tournament. Leo knew nothing about restricted choice, so when his opponent played the queen under Leo's king, Leo sat for a while in thought. Leo's cigar-smoking partner dozed off during the long huddle, and Leo looked up to see that some ashes from the cigar had ignited his partner's lapel. Leo leapt up and extinguished the blaze, meanwhile knocking North's cards onto the table and observing the club jack among them. The odds changed instantly, and Leo's problem was solved. The unhappy opponents called the tournament director, who ruled, "There is no penalty for putting out a fire in partner's suit."

Table 9-3 shows some common restricted-choice situations. The odds are computed on the assumption that East plays at random when he has to choose between cards of equal value to him. The third combination shows the value of the lowly eightspot. The obvious "alternative" to the recommended play is to finesse the jack, which is better than finessing the eightspot only when East held doubleton 10–9 originally. The eightspot play is better when East's ten (or nine) is singleton. (Playing the king is always inferior, for the reasons given in discussing king-jack-nine-x opposite ace-x-x-x.) Since a specific 3–2 break is 12/10 as likely as a specific 4–1 break, East is dealt the 10-9 six times for each five times he is dealt the lone ten (or nine). But he plays the ten only three of those times, so the odds are 5 to 3 that his play of the ten was from a singleton holding, and South can dazzle the other players by successfully finessing the eight-spot.

Notice that the odds favoring these plays are all much heavier than those favoring the usual "book" plays, so they are well worth learning.

How the Odds Change

Let's return now to Table 9-2. The odds in column three are based on absolutely no knowledge of the distribution of the other suits. But what if we knew, from the play of the other suits, that East had been dealt nine cards in spades and hearts, and West, only three? Then, in a, East would have only four chances to hold the club king, and West would have nine. The "book" play of the ace would be suicide, bucking 9 to 4 adverse odds. To make the finesse the favorite here, East only has to have fewer slots for the king than West has, and this will be true if you know he was dealt two more cards than West in some other suit(s). The other cases in the table can be worked out in similar fashion, using only the ability to count up to thirteen.

Case g gives you a chance to make an unusual, but sound, play. If you lead a small card from South, and West plays small, only the king and jack are unseen. The book play is the queen, rather than the ace, because West is more likely, on the principle of restricted choice, to have held king-x rather than jack-x. (With jack-x he might have played the jack; with king-x, his play would be automatic.) But the finesse of the ten, which succeeds against West's holding of king-jack-x, is not so bad as a second choice. The odds favoring king-x over king-jack-x are only 13 to 11, and a little information can change these odds dramatically. Suppose you know that West was dealt only one spade, and East six. On the times when West holds the king-x of clubs, he still has ten slots for the jack, while East has only seven; thus the finesse of the ten is better than the finesse of the queen, by odds of 10 to 7.

How does this sort of reasoning work in a whole hand? Try this one:

	Spades	Hearts	Diamonds	Clubs
North:	x x x	A x x	x x x x	K x x
South:	A K Q	K x x	A K J 10 x	A x

West leads a spade against South's six no trump. South cashes a second spade to see what happens, and East discards a club. The ace of diamonds brings small ones from East and West, and both opponents follow suit when a club is played to the king. East plays low on the next diamond; what should South do?

This is not the time to make a book play or recite slogans. West has only six slots for the diamond queen, and East has ten, so the finesse is a 10 to 6 favorite to bring in the slam.[2]

Odds in the Bidding

Rubber Bridge

In rubber bridge, the value of your result is not immediately entered on the score sheet. A part score carries with it an increased expectation of winning a game; a game gives you a better chance of winning the rubber and thus collecting the rubber bonus. These expectations are incorporated into the figures in table 9-4, which shows the estimated value of various results when you have bid under game, game, small slam, or grand slam.

When you bid a slam, the slam bonus is scored immediately, but the value of the game does not appear until the rubber is over. The approximate value of the game can be found from the value of the rubber. After you win the first game, you will score 700 if you win the second game. If you

Table 9-4. Values of Various Results at Rubber Bridge

Amount bid (major suit)	Points for winning				
	Nine tricks	Ten tricks	Eleven tricks	Twelve tricks	Thirteen tricks
Both vulnerable					
3	+ 215	+ 245	+ 275	+ 305	+ 335
4	− 100	+ 620	+ 650	+ 680	+ 710
6	− 300	− 200	− 100	+ 1,430	+ 1,460
7	− 400	− 300	− 200	− 100	+ 2,210
Vulnerable vs. non-vulnerable					
3	+ 190	+ 220	+ 250	+ 280	+ 310
4	− 100	+ 520	+ 550	+ 580	+ 610
6	− 300	− 200	− 100	+ 1,330	+ 1,360
7	− 400	− 300	− 200	− 100	+ 2,110
Not vulnerable					
3	+ 165	+ 195	+ 225	+ 255	+ 285
4	− 50	+ 420	+ 450	+ 480	+ 510
6	− 150	− 100	− 50	+ 980	+ 1,010
7	− 200	− 150	− 100	− 50	+ 1,510

lose the second game, your chances of winning or losing the rubber are equal, so it would seem that the net value of that first game is 50% of 700, or 350. However, becoming vulnerable may cost you some points in penalties, so it is generally considered that the first game is worth only 300, and the game that wins you a two-game rubber is therefore worth the remaining 400. Obviously, winning the deciding game in a three-game rubber is worth 500 points.

Experts differ on the value of a part score. Weighing all the arguments leads one to a part-score value of about one-quarter of a game—that is, 75 points not vulnerable, 100 points when you are vulnerable against nonvulnerable opponents, and 125 points when both sides are vulnerable. Thus, for example, table 9-4 lists 215 as the value of three spades bid and made—90 points on the score sheet and 125 points for the value of the part score—when both sides are vulnerable.

We can use this table to work out the criteria for a profitable slam or game bid. In all situations, we see that a game bid stands to gain more than it loses. For example, if nine tricks are sure and ten tricks are possible, bidding a vulnerable game costs you 315 points [the difference between + 215 and − 100] when you fail, and it gains 375 [the difference between + 620 and + 245] when you succeed. [We ignore the possibility of being doubled, which makes the game bid less attractive when your trumps are weak.]

.The exact ratio of these numbers is of little significance. You should simply try to bid a game when you have about a 50% or better chance of making it. How do you know when you have a 50% chance? Usually you don't know during the bidding. People who claim that their bidding system is that precise are not to be taken seriously. But you can make a mental note of the game bids that appear to be close decisions and then keep track of how many you actually make. If you make significantly more than half of your "doubtful" game bids, you are not bidding enough of them. Even if these bids are not technically sound, the fact that your opponents are letting you make them justifies the bidding of game on them. On the other hand, if you make significantly fewer than 50% of those games, you are either overbidding them or underplaying them. In either case, pull in your horns.

The odds that count are the odds that exist when you make your bid, not the odds after you see both hands. In some cases you are perfectly justified in staying out of a game that turns out to be a 100% chance. For example, suppose that making the game requires that your partner hold two specific honor cards, and from the bidding you know that he holds about one-third of the missing strength. In such a case, he has only one chance in three to have any specific honor card, and it is distinctly a losing bet to bid the game. But if you can't stand the embarrassment of failing to bid the game when he does have that magic hand, then go ahead and bid it. It's your money.

The same logic applies to slam bidding. In most cases you need a 50% chance of success to break even on a slam bid. This does not mean that [to quote one best-selling bridge book] a small slam "should" be bid when there is a 50% chance to make it. Rather, you should bid it when it appears to be 50%

at worst, and you should stay out of it if it appears to be 50% *at best*. For example, if you find that your side is missing the king of trumps as well as one ace, you have nothing to gain by plunging ahead into slam. Sometimes, in such cases, you will make twelve tricks via a successful trump finesse, and your partner will ask, "How should we have bid it?" The answer is that you can't bid your opponents' cards [unless they tell you what they have].

However, it does pay in the long run to bid a 50% small slam if you already have a part score. In that case you have already "won" about a quarter of a game, so an unsuccessful slam bid costs you, besides trick score and penalty, only an average of three-quarters of a game. In the best case, when you are vulnerable and opponents are not, you risk only 550 points to gain an additional 750, so you can be bolder than usual.

Far more caution is called for where grand slams are concerned. In general, if twelve tricks are sure, a seven bid risks about twice as much as it stands to gain, so it is not a good bet unless it is a 2 to 1 favorite to succeed. But the situation changes drastically if the opponents attempt a sacrifice bid.

If East–West bid seven clubs over North–South's six-spade bid, the profit that could have been made in six spades becomes irrelevant. All that matters then is the penalty for defeating seven clubs, relative to the expectation for a seven-spade bid. If the distribution is highly unbalanced, the penalty can be paltry, compared to the reward for bringing home a grand slam. A probability of only 30% of scoring 2,210 gives you a net expectation of 590 points [30% of + 2,210 plus 70% of − 100]. This is better than claiming a 500-point penalty, and it makes the game more interesting as well. [Granted, it might be hard to explain to your partner why you made him play a scary grand slam when a sure profit was available on defense.]

You can work out the profit-and-loss figures yourself for accepting sacrifice bids at other levels. When you get down to the five level, you need a much bigger probability of making your bid to justify passing up the penalty. Bidding five hearts to score 650, when a 500-point penalty of the opponents was a sure thing, only breaks even when the probability of success is a hefty 80%.

Duplicate Bridge

The odds discussed above are not relevant to duplicate bridge, where you don't care how much profit you make on a hand, but rather how often you figure to make even a small extra profit relative to what other players are making in your position. So your strategy must depend somewhat on what you expect other players to do with your cards and with your opponents' cards.

Suppose you are in a duplicate game with a bunch of rabbits who will never make a sacrifice bid. Your opponents, curse the luck, turn out to be the only tigers in the room; they bid five clubs over your iron-clad vulnerable four-spade bid. If you have assessed the other players correctly, scoring a 500-point penalty on this hand will be worth absolutely nothing, because all the other players with your cards will be playing a game in spades, scoring 620 or 650. Therefore, having the courage of your convictions, you bid five spades, because you can't do any worse than get a zero anyway.

Even if you expect several pairs to find the sacrifice bid, you should go on to five spades on hands that would not justify that bid at rubber bridge. Suppose the hand is played at twelve other tables; at six of them, East and West go down 500 in five clubs, and at the other six, your North–South counterparts score an uncontested vulnerable game. If you score 500, you tie six pairs and get three match points [out of a possible twelve]. If you bid five spades, you get nine match points when it makes and zero when it fails. In the long run, the five-spade bid breaks even if its chance of success is only 1 in 3! [But it is not such a good proposition if a 700-point penalty is possible, or if other parts might miss the game with your cards.]

IMP Scoring

The paragraphs on duplicate bridge do not apply to the team-of-four games in which the scoring is done by "international match points" [IMPs]. In such a game, the IMP score on each hand depends on the difference between the scores at the two tables, making the rewards more like those in rubber bridge. If you decline an offer of 500 points in order to play for 650, the 150 points that you may gain will be worth 4 IMPs, but the 600-point loss that you risk will cost 12 IMPs. In the years when Italy won world championships with monotonous regularity, they gained bushels of points from American teams who, being more accustomed to pair scoring, often "took the push" to the five level and converted a plus 500 into a minus 100.

General Principles of Competitive Bidding

It is all very well to say what chance of success is needed to make any given bid profitable, but how do you assess that chance during the bidding, especially on the unbalanced, competitive hands that create the most problems?

There is no way that a book can tell you how an expert would figure the odds on such hands. He would probably rely on his past experience with his partner of the moment on similar hands. But there is one general rule that can be very helpful to you. The following hand will illustrate the rule:

	Spades	Hearts	Diamonds	Clubs
North:	x x x	A x x	x	x x x x x x
South:	A K Q x x x x	x x	x x	x x

North–South will almost certainly take nine tricks with spades as trumps, but East–West can take eleven if diamonds are trumps. The sum of these numbers is called the total trick count. In a surprisingly large number of hands, this total is equal to the sum of the number of cards in North–South's longest suit (spades, ten cards) and the number of cards in East–West's longest suit (diamonds, ten cards); that these totals should be equal is called the "Rule of Total Tricks."

Obviously, the rule is not perfect. If you take away an offensive trick from North–South without taking away a defensive trick, for example, by changing the spades to x-x-x opposite ace-x-x-x-x-x, the rule fails. But its virtue is that it works in the more frequent situations where the strength of each side is in its long suits, and the short suits break normally.

The rule of total tricks allows you to play the odds instead of fretting over things that you don't know, and can't possibly know. For example, your LHO opens with one spade, your partner doubles, and your RHO bids four spades. What should you do with:

Spades	Hearts	Diamonds	Clubs
x x	A x x x x x	x x	x x x

Your partner figures to have four hearts, and the opponents are bidding as if they have ten spades, so the total trick count is twenty. If they can't make four spades, you can make five hearts. If your partner has, say,

Spades	Hearts	Diamonds	Clubs
x	K x x x	A x x x	K Q x x

four spades is probably unbeatable, but five hearts is a good sacrifice. Give your partner the diamond king instead of his small one, and you will beat four spades, but you will also make five hearts if the club ace is where it should be.

On the other side of the coin, if you are not particularly long in trumps, you should be wary of competing at high levels. When the total trick count is around seventeen and you have enough power to make your own contract, you can probably devastate their game-level bid. If the opponents bid four spades over your four-heart bid, you should not even consider bidding five hearts. If they can make ten tricks, you figure to go down four in five hearts; and if you can make five hearts, then they will be down four in four spades.

The total trick rule also shows why you can pick up a windfall by doubling the opponents at a low level (more so than when a high level has been reached and the opponents have had a better chance to assess their trump fit). If an opponent sticks his neck out by overcalling on a five-card suit, he could find his partner with a singleton. They might have difficulty finding a better suit, and your own side may have no suit whose combined length is more than seven. This means that you can probably take as many tricks playing the hand in their suit as playing it in your own suit! Winning nine tricks in your suit gives you a part-score, but winning nine tricks in their suit yields a four-trick penalty at the two-level.

Conclusion

The use of probabilities in bridge does not mean memorizing mathematical tables or ignoring what is going on at the bridge table. On the contrary, the more you observe what is bid and what is played, the more intelligently you can assess the probabilities when you have to make a decision. Furthermore, this assessment does not require complicated mental arithmetic. Usually all you need is the ability to count up to thirteen.

CHAPTER 10

Poker

In TV shows, poker is always presented as a game of either luck or bluff. Obviously, it has those elements, but luck and bluff won't get you very far if you don't know the probabilities. Oswald Jacoby[1] has said that poker actually has a smaller element of luck than any other card game, including bridge, because in poker you are able to limit your losses on a run of bad hands. And the bluff is only effective when used in moderation; an all-out bluff always risks more than it stands to gain.

As in other card games, a player whose habits were one hundred percent predictable would be at a big disadvantage as soon as the other players figured him out, so a little bluffing is essential. Computers that have been programmed to play the odds and to draw inferences from other players actions have also been programmed to bluff.[2] They must be really tough opponents; they never have to worry about keeping a poker face. [One classmate of mine was said to have a perfect poker face—and he put it on whenever he had a good hand!]

But it is not my purpose to teach poker strategy. There are a huge number of poker variations, and I am in no position to give advice on all of them. So let us just see how probabilities can be a general guide to the right decision.

Poker Expectations

In poker, as in any other gamble, the important quantity is your expectation, or average return. If this is higher than the amount you have to bet in order to call, then you have an "overlay," and you should stay in. Otherwise, fold. Obviously, you can't always compute the expectation on the spot, but focusing on your expectation helps you to avoid many mistakes.

The biggest mistake is to think that some of the money in the pot belongs to you. That money ceased to be yours the moment you threw it into the pot. All that matters now is how much more you have to put in and how much you are buying for it. [An extension of this mistake is to refuse to quit playing when you are behind because you think "I have to get my money back." As we saw in chapter 2, what you have already lost is no longer your money, and it has absolutely nothing to do with your future expectations. If it has any effect at all, it is the negative psychological effect of being a loser. Yet the winners are the ones who always want to quit, and the losers won't let them.]

Odds Offered by the Pot

Let's look at one situation that does allow you to figure your expectation. In draw poker, you are last to speak, the pot holds $11, and you must bet $2 to call [before the draw]. You hold spades: king-jack-9-7; hearts: ace. You have nine chances of drawing a spade out of forty-seven possible cards. If you do draw that spade, your flush will win about 90% of the time [in a five- or six-player game, according to the figures in table 10-3], so your chance of winning the pot is about 8/47. This means that your $2 "investment" buys you 8/47 of the $13 pot, or about $2.20. You don't mind buying $2.20 for $2, so you stay.

Granted, there are some complications even here in such a simple case. If you fail to get your flush, your $2 is gone, and that's that. But when you succeed, you may still have to invest more money to claim your pot. That shouldn't worry you, though, because you know that your flush should win about 90% of the time. Additional betting should only increase your expectation, as long as you don't drop a bundle on the one hand in ten that is a loser.

Odds in Draw Poker

To have any chance of correctly estimating your expectation in situations like the above, you have to know the probability that your hand will beat the other hands. In figuring this probability, you obviously can't afford to ignore the way the other players are betting, but you have to begin with the a priori probability of getting a hand as good as your own. If you know that, then you can make adjustments for the information that you get from other players' bets. It is true that many players after playing a large number of hands acquire a "feel" for the value of a hand without formally learning a priori probabilities. But the trial-and-error method can be expensive when the errors occur.

We begin with the odds on the dealt hand even though the hand is often improved by the draw, because the best hand before the draw has to be the favorite to win the pot eventually. (But this does not mean that it is an odds-on favorite.) Table 10-1 shows the number of ways to deal each of the possible five-card poker hands. It also shows, for any given hand, the probability that a better hand will be dealt to one of the other players (for one to six other players).

The first column in the table is not directly useful, but it is used to construct the numbers in the other columns. For example, the fact that there are 84,480 ways to be dealt a pair of aces is not in itself significant; but by adding all the numbers above this, you can find that there are 198,180 hands better than a pair of aces out of 2,598,960 possible hands. This gives a probability of roughly 198,180/1,598,960, or about 7.6%, that any given player can beat your pair of aces. (The word *roughly* is used because these would be the exact odds only if each opponent's hand were drawn from a full deck. The fact that you know what five cards you hold changes the odds a bit; for example, it makes it very unlikely

Table 10-1. Ways to Deal Five-Card Poker Hands

Hand	Number of ways	Probability that opponent has a better hand[a] when the number of opposing hands is:					
		1	2	3	4	5	6
Straight flush	40	0	0	0	0	0	0
Four of a kind	624	.00002	.00003	.00005	.00006	.00008	.00009
Full house	3,744	.00026	.00051	.00078	.00102	.00128	.00153
Flush	5,108	.00170	.00339	.00509	.00677	.00847	.01015
Straight	10,200	.00366	.00731	.01094	.01457	.01817	.02177
Three of a kind	54,912	.00759	.01511	.02259	.03000	.03736	.04466
Two pairs:							
Aces high	19,008	.02871	.05660	.08369	.11001	.13556	.16038
Kings	17,424	.03603	.07076	.10424	.13651	.16762	.19761
Queens	15,840	.04273	.08364	.12280	.16028	.19617	.23052
Jacks	14,256	.04883	.09527	.13945	.18146	.22143	.25945
Tens	12,672	.05431	.10568	.15425	.20019	.24362	.28470
Nines	11,088	.05919	.11487	.16726	.21655	.26292	.30655
Eights	9,504	.06345	.12288	.17854	.23067	.27948	.32520
Sevens	7,920	.06711	.12972	.18812	.24261	.29344	.34086
Sixes	6,336	.07016	.13540	.19606	.25246	.30491	.35367
Fives	4,752	.07260	.13992	.20236	.26027	.31397	.36378
Fours	3,168	.07443	.14331	.20707	.26608	.32071	.37126
Threes	1,584	.07564	.14556	.21019	.26993	.32515	.37620

Table 10-1. continued

Hand	Number of ways	Probability that opponent has a better hand[a] when the number of opposing hands is:					
		1	2	3	4	5	6
One pair:							
Aces	84,480	.07625	.14669	.21176	.27187	.32739	.37868
Kings	"	.10876	.20569	.29208	.36907	.43769	.49885
Queens	"	.14126	.26257	.36674	.45620	.53302	.59899
Jacks	"	.17377	.31734	.43597	.53398	.61496	.68187
Tens	"	.20627	.37000	.49995	.60310	.68497	.74995
Nines	"	.23878	.42054	.55891	.66423	.74441	.80544
Eights	"	.27129	.46898	.61303	.71801	.79451	.85026
Sevens	"	.30379	.51529	.66254	.76506	.83643	.88612
Sixes	"	.33630	.55950	.70764	.80596	.87121	.91452
Fives	"	.36880	.60159	.74852	.84127	.89981	.93676
Fours	"	.40131	.64157	.78541	.87153	.92309	.95395
Threes	"	.43381	.67943	.81850	.89724	.94182	.96706
Deuces	"	.46632	.71518	.84800	.91888	.95671	.97690
No pair	1,302,540	.49882	.74882	.87411	.93691	.96838	.98415
All hands	2,598,960						

a. Assuming that you have the best hand of its type—for example, ace-high if you have no pair.

that somebody else holds a pair of aces. But the overall change in the odds is very small.]

The numbers in the remaining columns of table 10-1 are derived from the probability that one player can beat you. Since there is a probability of .964 that one player cannot beat that pair of aces, the probability that neither one of two players can beat it is [.924]², or about .853, making a probability of .147 that one of the two can beat it. For six opposing hands, the probability that the aces will not be topped is [.924]⁶, or 62.1%, making the probability 37.9% that they will be beaten.

These numbers are the basis for the book advice on minimum requirements for an opening bet. The conservative [tight] policy is not to open unless there is about a 50% chance that you have the best hand. Thus it is a good general rule always to open with kings or better; even as the first bettor in a seven-handed game you have a 50% chance that yours is the best hand at that moment.

With a pair of jacks, a "tight" player will open only if there are four or fewer players yet to speak. You see from table 10-1 that this gives him a 47% [or better] chance of having the best hand. When there are five players to be heard from, that chance shrinks to 38%.

Odds after the Draw

This criterion—that is, you should open only when you have about a 50% chance of having the best hand—gives you a sound start. But you must remember that having the best hand before the draw is no guarantee of success. Table 10-2 shows the chances of improving your hand on the draw. You see that your chance of improving a pair is only about 29%. But with four opponents, each with a 29% chance of improvement, there is a probability of 74% that at least one of them will improve.[3] This means that, even if you start with the best pair and therefore have a better chance than any other player, your chance of winning the pot is still considerably less than 50%.

Table 10-2. Probabilities of Improving a Poker Hand on the Draw (Exact probability and approximate odds against)

Cards held	Improvement to:				
	Two pairs	*Three of a kind*	*Full house*	*Four of a kind*	*Total*
One pair	864/5405 5 to 1	618/5405 31 to 4	11/1081 97 to 1	3/1081 359 to 1	1552/5405 5 to 2
One pair and kicker	186/1081 19 to 4	84/1081 12 to 1	9/1081 119 to 1	1/1081 1080 to 1	280/1081 20 to 7
Two pairs	—	—	4/47 11 to 1	—	4/47 11 to 1
Three of a kind	—	—	66/1081 31 to 2	2/47 45 to 2	112/1081 26 to 3
Three of a kind and kicker	—	—	3/47 15 to 1	1/47 46 to 1	4/47 11 to 1
	Straight	*Flush*	*Straight flush*		*Straight or better*
Inside straight	4/47 11 to 1				4/47 11 to 1
Open-ended straight	8/47 5 to 1	—			8/47 5 to 1
Four-flush	—	9/47 17 to 4	—		9/47 17 to 4
Inside straight flush	3/47 15 to 1	8/47 5 to 1	1/47 46 to 1		12/47 3 to 1
Open-ended straight flush	6/47 7 to 1	7/47 6 to 1	2/47 45 to 2		15/47 2 to 1

The "Loose" Game

Many players find it boring to throw in a hand as often as the "tight" policy demands. Such players may play the completely "loose" style of staying in the pot (or opening, when permitted) on any hand that contains a pair or better. This policy is not too costly if the ante is fairly large relative to the normal bet. The presence of one or two loose players in the game induces the others to loosen up, since the pot offers bigger rewards.

After another player has opened, you should stay if you think your hand is as good as his minimum opener. To judge this, you might count how often he opens in first position. A tight player will open only about one hand in seven; this is how often he holds a pair of kings or better [table 10-1]. A player who opens about half of the time is obviously opening on any pair.

Probabilities after the Draw

Table 10-3 shows frequencies of various hands after the draw, on the assumption of a completely loose game, with players staying in on any pair as well as on open-ended straights and four-flushes. In constructing the table it was assumed that a player would prefer to keep a pair of jacks or better instead of saving an open straight or a four-flush, but that he would break up a low pair to draw to an open straight or four-flush.

The number of hands that result from these assumptions is found by adding up all ways of arriving at each final hand starting with the original holdings and their frequencies. For example, to finish with three of a kind, you could start with three of a kind and fail to improve, or you could draw one matching card to a pair. There are 54,912 original holdings of three of a kind, and 43/47 of these [50,239] fail to improve. [We assume that a kicker is always held, but this assumption has little effect on the overall result.] There are 1,051,714 holdings that are *played* as a pair [46,526 pair hands contain a potential straight or flush with a low pair that is broken up], and 618/5,405 of these [120,251] improve to three of a kind. This makes a total of 170,490 final hands, or 11.89% of all *played* hands, that hold three of a kind.

From these percentages we can tell how good a hand will usually win in this kind of game. A pair of queens has about a 50% chance to win against one other player, since about 50% of played hands are worse than that. To have a 50% chance against two other players, you need about a 71% chance to beat each one; this requires at least two pairs, tens high. And to have at least a 50% probability of beating four opponents, you need about an 84% chance against each one, which requires at least three fours. [Three fours will lose to 10/13 of all hands having three of a kind—about 130,000 hands—plus the 82,000 hands with straight or better, or about 15% of all played hands.]

You must remember that these numbers are only averages and are intended as a general guide to hand evaluation. They take no account of the level of the betting or of tendencies of later bettors to adjust their standards according to the number of players already in the pot. Also remember that the table applies only to a loose game and has little relevance to a tight game.

Adjustments to the Probabilities

In interpreting tables like these, you must also keep in mind the assumption that each person's hand has been dealt from a full deck. You know that the deck from which your opponents' hands were drawn is missing certain cards—the cards you have been looking at—and this knowledge is often very useful. For example, an original hand including a pair of queens, a king, and an ace is actually stronger [slightly] than a hand with only a pair of kings, and you can treat it as a pair of kings for openers.[4]

Suppose you draw to your pair of queens and you are lucky enough to catch a third queen. You can back these three queens as strongly as you would normally bet on three aces, because it is very unlikely that anyone will beat you with three of a kind. There is only one three-ace combination and one three-king combination for an opponent to hold instead of the usual four of each. So even though you no longer hold that king [or ace], you benefit by knowing that nobody else holds it, either.

Odds In Stud Poker

Stud poker somehow seems to encourage more speculative betting than draw poker. It is hard to give up on a hand after seeing only two cards. But the winners are the ones who can

Table 10-3. Frequencies of Hands after the Draw in a Loose Game[a]

Final hand	Original cards kept	Number of original hands	Probability of final hand	Number of final hands	Percentage of played hands
Straight flush	Straight flush	40	1	40	
	Open straight flush	1,188	2/47	51	
	Inside straight flush	4,608	1/47	98	0.013
Four of a kind	Four of a kind	624	1	624	
	Three of a kind	54,912	1/47	1,168	
	One pair	1,051,714	3/1,081	2,919	0.329
Full house	Full house	3,744	1	3,744	
	Three of a kind	54,912	3/47	3,505	
	Two pairs	123,552	4/47	10,515	
	One pair	1,051,714	11/1,081	10,702	1.99
Flush	Flush	5,108	1	5,108	
	Open straight flush	1,188	7/47	177	
	Inside straight flush	4,608	8/47	784	
	Common four-flush	95,030	9/47	18,194	1.69

Table 10-3. continued

Final hand	Original cards kept	Number of original hands	Probability of final hand	Number of final hands	Percentage of played hands
Straight	Straight	10,200	1	10,200	
	Open straight flush	1,188	6/47	152	
	Inside straight flush	4,608	3/47	294	
	Open straight	82,800	8/47	14,094	1.73
Three of a kind	Three of a kind	54,912	43/47	50,239	
	One pair	1,051,714	618/5,405	120,251	11.89
Two pairs	Two pairs	123,552	43/47	113,037	
	One pair	1,051,714	864/5,405	168,119	19.61
One	One pair	1,051,714	3,853/5,405	749,723	
	Four-flushes	100,826	[note b]	25,228	
	Open straight	82,800	[note b]	20,666	55.50
No pair	Four-flushes	100,826		55,845	
	Open straight	82,800		48,040	7.25

a. Assumptions: [1] all pairs, four-flushes, and open straights are played; [2] kicker is always kept with three of a kind; and [3] pair of jacks or better is kept rather than a four-flush, but possible straight flushes are kept.

b. Probability varies; it is 11/47 if original hand had a pair.

make those hard decisions. The sound policy is to stay in at any stage only if you can beat what is showing on the board. If your two cards can't beat an opponent's one card, you are a distinct underdog, and you should save your money for something better.

The frequencies of dealt hands in five-card stud poker are the same as in draw poker [table 10-1], and they serve as a rough guide at the beginning of the hand. For example, if your first two cards are a pair of deuces, you know that you must improve to win the pot; in a six-handed game, a pair of deuces is high about 2% of the time. Nevertheless, any pair is better than no pair, and only one hand in seventeen begins with a pair in the first two cards. You should back your pair until events convince you that you are up against a superior hand.

Effect of the "Board" on the Odds

The other players' face-up cards—the cards on the "board"—provide information that can drastically affect the probabilities for your own hand as well as their hands. For example, in a six-handed game, that hand starting with two deuces will end up as the best hand almost 29% of the time—provided that no other deuce is showing on the board at the beginning. If a deuce is showing, that 29% plunges to 24%. I'll let you work out those figures for yourself, using the tables in this chapter.

Betting on Hopes

Let's now look at the development of the hand. Having seen that you "beat the board," you have taken a third card. Again, you should stay in only if there is a reasonable chance that you have the best hand at this point, and you must ask yourself why the other players are staying in. There are too many possibilities to tabulate here, but the point is to bet on values in hand, not on hopes.

Here is an example of betting on hopes. For some reason you have decided to draw another card to the nine and 10 of Hearts, and you catch the eight of Hearts. Now you have all sorts of possibilities: flush, straight, straight flush—even two pairs or three of a kind. By now you have seen, say, eight cards on the board, and by some remarkable stroke of luck, none of them is one that would have helped you. Under these highly favorable conditions, what is your chance of bringing in one of your possibilities?

There are 820 ways of selecting two cards from the forty-one that you haven't seen, and 126 of these will give you two pairs or better (count them yourself). So the odds against you are 694 to 126—almost 6 to 1. You have a small bluffing possibility if you draw, say, a six and a five so that you have a possible straight showing. But if you want to save money, just fold now. This is the time to remind yourself that the money in the pot is no longer yours. Obviously, your chances are even slimmer if one or more of the cards you could use is on the table—as it usually is in this situation.

A similar calculation can be applied to the oddball draw of two cards to this holding in draw poker. The only difference is that there are forty-seven cards that you haven't seen instead of forty-one. This gives 1,081 ways to draw two cards (47 x 46/2), while you still have only 126 ways to improve your hand. So the odds against you are 955 to 126—more than 7.5 to 1.

Seven-card Stud

In this game, the winning hand naturally tends to be better—usually three of a kind or two pairs, aces high, in contrast to the high pair that you expect to be a winner in five-card stud (as shown in table 10-1). But this average winning hand has less relevance to the betting problems that you face. You must concentrate on deducing what you can about the concealed cards. You can speculate more because your chances of improvement are so great, but when you do, you should be ready to drop out fast.

It is reasonable to stay in on a three-flush as long as no other card of that suit is showing. In a six-handed game, you then have a 22% chance of filling the flush; but if even one of your suit is showing on the board, your chance drops to 18%. If your fourth card does not fit or give you a high pair, it is time to quit. Your chance of filling the flush is down to 16% if no card of your suit is showing on the board and 13% if one card is showing, as will usually be the case.

The tables and principles discussed in this chapter can be applied to the many other varieties of poker. It is now up to you to work them out for yourself. If you want more detailed information, read a complete book, such as *Oswald Jacoby on Poker*, mentioned earlier in this chapter.

CHAPTER 11

Other Friendly Games

There are many games with somewhat limited mathematical aspects, but which are nevertheless worth exploring. Do you know which type of discard is safest in gin rummy? Do you know when to accept a double in backgammon? Do you know which is the most profitable set of properties in Monopoly? Do you know when to concede a pinochle hand after you have bought the widow? If not, read on.

Gin Rummy

Like the other games that we are discussing here, gin rummy has many aspects that can't be dealt with mathematically. But at the beginning of the hand, mathematics is just about all you have to go on. A great deal of this has to do with finding a safe discard.

As in many other odds problems, the choosing of a safe discard is just a matter of counting the possibilities. If you have no other information, there are from two to six combinations that your discard can fill for your opponent. In order of increasing danger, your discards and the number of combinations that they fill are:

Discard	Number of combinations it fills
Ace or king from a pair	2
Queen or two from a pair	3
Lone ace or king	4

Jack through three from a pair	4
Lone queen or two	5
Lone jack through three	6

For example, the heart jack could fill: spade jack, diamond jack; spade jack, club jack; diamond jack, club jack; heart king and queen; or heart ten and nine.

After your opponent has discarded, the safety of your own discards obviously depends on what he has thrown. But do you know *how* safe a given discard becomes as a result of his play[s]? It is important to be precise, for there is a huge percentage difference between a three-way player and a four-way player—the difference is much bigger than your bookie's percentage. For example, a lone eight is normally a six-way player, but if your opponent throws an eight, you know that he does not have a pair of eights left. Therefore it becomes only a three-way player—it can fill the ten-nine, the nine-seven, or the seven-six in the same suit.

This does not mean, however, that this eight is a safe discard. Your opponent may be ''advertising.'' In the early game, he may deliberately throw, say, the club eight when he holds the nine and seven of hearts, hoping to induce a discard of the heart eight from you. In such a case you should, when the choice arises, throw a four-way player rather than respond to what might be an ad.

But you can rely on some information you get from your opponent's discards. The early discard of the club eight, for example, shows you that you can discard a nine or a seven of another suit in relative safety. Your opponent almost surely does not have the heart eight or the club seven, so the seven of hearts will fill only two likely combinations: six and five of hearts or one pair of sevens [diamonds and spades]. That makes this discard as safe as breaking up a pair of kings, as long as it is early in the hand.

So we have a general rule for the early game:

Your safest discard is of a rank adjacent to that of your opponent's last discard, but in a different suit.

Many players are unaware of this rule, and it seems paradoxical. When your opponent throws the six of hearts, the five of clubs becomes a safer discard than the five of hearts in the absence of other information. In fact the five of hearts is twice as dangerous, because it is a four-way player. [Work it out for yourself.]

Gin strategy involves a great deal more than safe discarding, and the discussion here covers only the early game. But most of the rest is a matter of paying careful attention to discards and drawing of proper inferences, so it is outside the scope of this book. For more advice on overall strategy, refer to *How to Be a Consistent Winner in the Most Popular Card Games*,[1] which has an excellent chapter on gin rummy.

Pinochle

Quite a few decisions in pinochle can be analyzed as straight percentage propositions. To illustrate, let us follow the rules for three-handed auction pinochle, as follows:

1. The basic values for each bid are:

300 to 340	3 chips
350 to 390	5 chips
400 to 440	10 chips
450 to 490	15 chips
500 to 540	20 chips
550 to 590	25 chips
600 or more	30 chips

2. If any suit except spades is trump, the successful bidder collects the basic value from each of the other players, plus the kitty; if spades are trumps, he collects twice the basic value from each of these sources.

3. A bidder may concede defeat before leading to the first trick by paying each player and the kitty the basic value of his bid, regardless of the suit named as trump.

4. A bidder who plays and then fails to make his bid is "double bete." He pays double the amount that he would have collected for a successful bid [which would be four times the basic value, to each player and the kitty, if spades are trumps].

Local rules vary on payments to the kitty for bids below 350, so we shall just consider bids of 350 or more.

Odds in the Bidding

The scoring table described above severely punishes over-bidding [although you'd never know it from the bidding in a typical game]. It is a losing proposition to risk a sure 350 for 400 unless the odds are 5 to 1 in favor of making the 400.[2] You can figure these odds yourself by simple arithmetic. The reward for 400 is 30 chips [10 each from the other players and the kitty], but failing to make it costs you 60 chips. To equal the expectation of 15 chips that you had with your sure bid of 350, you need to win 30 chips on five hands out six. This will give you 150 chips minus the 60 you lose on the sixth hand, or 90 chips on six hands—15 per hand.

Higher bids risk even more; the odds required are shown below [on the assumption that a lower bid is sure to make]. All odds apply to spades as well as the other suits.

Amount bid:	400	450	500	550	600
Odds needed:	5 to 1	8 to 1	11 to 1	14 to 1	17 to 1

But there is some encouragement for you overbidders. These figures apply only when you are sure to make the lower bid, and it is obviously a different story if you must bid higher to win the bid. If your opponent is likely to be bidding on a spade suit, you can be quite bold. If he bids 340 and you judge that he is almost sure to make it, you are going to lose 6 chips anyway. By bidding 350 you gain 21 chips [the difference between plus 15 and minus 6] when you succeed, and you lose an additional 24 when you fail, so it is almost an even-money proposition.

Playing or Conceding

Another factor that can reduce the punishment for over-bidding is the possibility of conceding after seeing the widow. Let's say that you have several possibilities for help in the widow, and you will concede if you find no help there. Then a bid of 400 [when 350 is a sure thing] will break even if the odds are "only" 3 to 1 in favor of your finding what you need. You will win 30 chips three times and lose 30 chips once for a net gain of 60 chips—the same amount you would have won by taking your sure 15 chips each time for a bid of 350.

This raises the question of how to decide whether to play or concede after you have seen the widow. If spades are trumps, you play if you decide that you have an even chance or better; in other suits you should play whenever you have a mere one chance in three of making it. You can confirm this advice for yourself by inspecting the table. For example, in spades the difference between making and conceding is exactly the same as the difference between conceding and going "double bete," so obviously you have an even-money bet and you can play on a 50% chance. In borderline cases, you should play because of the chance that your opponents will slip up [of course the chance that *you* will slip up is negligible]. In the following pages we'll see how you go about estimating your chance of making your bid after you have seen the widow.

Odds on Finding Cards in the Widow

You may have wondered how you could figure that you had odds of 3 to 1 in favor of finding help in the widow in the example just discussed. It is not too easy to do that from scratch while you are playing, but there are a few guidelines that can help.

The first thing to remember is that it is generally foolish to expect to fill a meld with a card from the widow. If you have only one specific "place open" where the widow could give you a meld, your probability of success is 31/176, making the odds about 5 to 1 against you. [You can work this out from the probability of failure. Say that you need an ace of spades; the first spade ace fails you with a probability of 30/33, and the second, assuming that the first fails, will be lacking on 29 out of 32 occasions. So the overall probability of failure is 30/33 times 29/32, or 145/176.]

If more than one place is open, your chances improve, but not enough to be much of a factor in the bidding. The chances are:

Places open	Probability of getting at least one filler	Odds
1	31/176	5 to 1 against
2	901/2,728	2 to 1 against
3	2,531/5,456	7 to 6 against
4	789/1,364	4 to 3 in favor
5	3,685/5,456	2 to 1 in favor

With chances as slim as these and a scoring table that punishes overbidding, a bid on the hope of finding a meld is suicidal. Even when the odds favor you, they are not good enough to justify a bid. And when the odds do favor you, it means that you must be looking at four or five possible melds. One of these is likely to be something like forty jacks, a meld that costs you so much in playing strength that you should probably bury it anyway.

Prospects from the widow are not so black when you are looking for playing strength. You can figure on an average of 20 to 30 points from the widow, usually as a result of drawing an additional card in one of your long suits. If you have nine cards in your two longest suits, the odds are almost 6 to 1 in favor of finding one more in the widow. With ten, eleven, or twelve cards, the odds are:

Number of cards held:	Ten	Eleven	Twelve
Odds in your favor:	9 to 2	4 to 1	3 to 1

These are nice odds, but the points you figure to pick up should be considered only as a margin of safety on your first bid, allowing you to bid again with some confidence if an opponent boosts. [But obviously you should not always play supersafe on your first bid; you should not become stereo-typed as a player who will always go higher when pushed. It always pays to be unpredictable.]

Odds on Suit Breaks

You should always try to figure the odds on making your bid before you play a card, so you know whether to play or concede. The most important factor to consider is the suit-break probability. Suit-break probabilities for pinochle are included in table 9-1 [last column], but the exact percentages are of little use. You will do nicely if you just remember that an odd number of cards has better than a 60% chance to divide as evenly as possible, but four or six cards are quite unlikely to divide evenly.

From the information in table 9-1 it is clear that a spade hand that depends on an even break of four or six cards should be conceded, but a heart, diamond, or club hand should be played under those circumstances. The odds on a division of a suit also apply to the division of high cards within a suit. This division will determine how many high cards the opponents can load onto their tricks. For example, if you hold a bare king, the opponents can probably grab 25 or 26 points in the suit by playing ace-ace or ace-ten on your king. But if you are really lucky, they will get only 19, be-cause one opponent will have no ace or ten. This requires a 4-0 division of those four top cards, a division that occurs only 10% of the time. A more likely chance for a favorable break occurs when you hold two cards, say king-queen. If the aces and tens are divided either 3-1 or 4-0, you will lose only 43 or less instead of the maximum possible loss of 49. If making your bid depends on this good fortune, you should definitely not concede, even in spades, because the chance of either a 3-1 or a 4-0 break is 60%.

Monopoly

Any reader of this book has surely played Monopoly, and most of you probably thought it was a game of pure luck. But luck obviously involves probability, and if you know the probabilities you can improve your chances of winning, even in Monopoly.

You have no control over your landing place, so you have to be lucky to build up a monopoly by hitting the necessary properties. But if nobody acquires a monopoly, the game becomes long and tedious, and it is normal to trade properties so that each party gets a monopoly. Do you know which one to go for?

There are two factors involved here: [1] the ratio of money invested to rental returned and [2] the occupancy factor, or the number of times that your property will be hit. These are summarized in table 11-1, which shows a computer-generated result for the occupancy factor.

The product of the last two columns in the table gives you the overall rate of return on your investment; adding up these products for a whole color group gives an idea of the value of a monopoly in that color group. The high-rent dark blue monopoly [Boardwalk and Park Place] gives a sum of 1.18, but this is not nearly as good as the result for the moderately priced orange group [New York Ave., etc.], which yields an impressive 1.58 return. Even though the total amount invested is smaller, the orange group pays a higher total return on the average, as we can see by summing the products of columns three and five. The total for Boardwalk and Park Place is $1,200 plus $2,020, or $3,220, versus a total of $3,260 for the orange group. The reason for this is the high occupancy factor resulting from the large number of escaping jailbirds that hit the orange properties.

These results don't prove that the orange monopoly necessarily gives you the best chance to win, because other monopolies can kill off an opponent faster. You might expect the "cost effectiveness" of the orange monopoly to be less decisive when the money supply is large and that the dark blue monopoly would then have the edge because of its huge rents.

This expectation was borne out when our computer was programmed to play actual games. When the high-rent Boardwalk monopoly was pitted against the orange one and each player had a net worth of more than $4,000 [so that

Table 11-1. Monopoly Probabilities and Earnings Factors

Property	Cost of monopoly [including hotels]	Rent with hotels	Rent/Cost	Occupancy rate[a] [average = 1]
Mediterranean		$250	0.68	0.81
Baltic	$370	$450	1.22	0.80
Oriental		$550	0.51	0.82
Vermont	$1,070	$550	0.51	0.86
Connecticut		$600	0.56	0.86
St. Charles		$750	0.39	1.05
States	$1,940	$750	0.39	0.89
Virginia		$900	0.46	0.95
St. James		$950	0.46	1.04
Tennessee	$2,060	$950	0.46	1.18
New York		$1,000	0.49	1.15
Kentucky		$1,050	0.36	1.08
Indiana	$2,930	$1,050	0.36	1.02
Illinois		$1,100	0.38	1.22
Atlantic		$1,150	0.38	1.03
Ventnor	$3,050	$1,150	0.38	1.00
Marvin Gardens		$1,200	0.39	1.00
Pacific		$1,275	0.33	1.00
North Carolina	$3,920	$1,275	0.33	0.93
Pennsylvania		$1,400	0.36	0.92
Park Place		$1,500	0.55	0.80
Boardwalk	$2,750	$2,000	0.73	1.01
Reading Railroad		$200	0.25	1.12
Pennsylvania Railroad		$200	0.25	1.06

[*table continued on next page*]

Table 11-1. *continued*

Property	Cost of monopoly (including hotels)	Rent with hotels	Rent/Cost	Occupancy rate[a] (average = 1)
B&O Railroad	$800	$200	0.25	1.12
Short Line Railroad		$200	0.25	0.92
Electric Company		$70[b]	0.23[b]	1.05
Water Works	$300	$70[b]	0.23[b]	1.06

a. Determined by computer. The computer started a piece at "Go" and moved it, using a random number generator for dice throws, for 200,000 turns. It was programmed for sixteen "Chance" cards (including advances to Go, Reading Railroad, St. Charles Place, Illinois Ave., Boardwalk, nearest utility, and nearest railroad [two cards], plus "Go back three spaces" and "Go to jail"), as well as sixteen "Community Chest" cards, which also included an "Advance to Go" and a "Go to jail."

b. Average values.

hotels could be built and held], Boardwalk had the edge. But when the assets were smaller, the situation was reversed.

Buying the Boardwalk-Park Place combine, with two houses each, costs slightly more than buying the three orange properties with three houses each. But you get as much rent from each of those three properties as you do for Boardwalk or Park Place, and you collect that rent more often. The computer found that, as a result, the orange monopoly has as substantial advantage when the total assets for each side were $2,000 or less. In 150 games under these conditions, orange won 101. When the assets were somewhat larger [$3,000, $3,500, or $4,000], orange won only 97 of 200 games, with 22 draws [in which each player's assets built up beyond $10,000]. And when each player began with $4,500, orange won only 32 of 100, with 24 draws and 44 losses.

In other matchups, the computer found that these two monopolies are the most frequent winners. As table 11-1 sug-

Table 11-2. Chances of Hitting Points at Various Distances

Distance	Ways to hit	Odds against	Distance	Ways to hit	Odds against
1	11	25 to 11	7	6	5 to 1
2	12	2 to 1	8	6	5 to 1
3	14	11 to 7	9	5	31 to 5
4	14	11 to 7	10	3	11 to 1
5	15	7 to 5	11	2	17 to 1
6	17	19 to 17	12	3	11 to 1

gests, the red group [Illinois et al.] and the yellow group [Atlantic et al.] are the next best.

Backgammon

I assume that the reader of this section is familiar with the rules of backgammon, and I shall simply cover a few situations that are rewarding to the player who knows the probabilities.

Odds on Hitting a "Blot"

At most stages of the game, there is no way to calculate the actual winning chance that any given play gives you. Nevertheless, you should be familiar with the odds on throwing various numbers with two dice [chapter 1] so you can assess the immediate dangers of various alternatives, especially in cases where you are forced to leave a "blot."

The chance that a blot will be hit from any given point can be found simply by counting which of the thirty-six possible dice combinations can do it. For example, if the enemy man is six points away, he can hit you by rolling any of the eleven combinations containing a six on one die; in addition, if you have not "made" any of the points in between, he can hit you by rolling any of the five combinations that total six, or by rolling a pair of twos. The resulting total of seventeen combinations is listed in table 11-2, along with the results for other distances, on the assumption that all intermediate points are open. It should not be hard for you to make the corrections for cases in which one or more intermediate points are already made.

To take a simple case in which these odds come into play, suppose that you have made your own nine and ten points, and your opponent has a blot on your twelve point. You roll a 4 and a 1, forcing you to leave a blot on the enemy ten point (three points away from his blot), or on his eleven point (two points away from his blot).

From the table, the choice is clear. Leave it on his eleven point, where there are twelve ways to hit it instead of fourteen. In general, you can see that, for numbers below six, the lower number is harder to get; but for numbers above six, the higher number is tougher (except that twelve is easier than eleven).

Odds on Bearing Off

Fine players have been known to stub their toes by not paying proper attention to the odds on bearing off men from various positions. These are shown in table 11-3. But the precise numbers are not to be memorized; all that you need to learn is which positions to take when you have a choice. For example, you may have a roll that will leave you seven points away from victory and you may be able to choose among the positions 4 and 3, 5 and 2, or 6 and 1 for your two men. (Leaving one man seven points away is not to be considered; it is always better to get every man within six points of home). The table shows that 5 and 2 is by far the best choice. To help you remember what to do on choices like this, there are a few general rules:

1. It is always better to have both men on your home table.
2. Given that, it is better to bear off one man if possible.
3. As long as you avoid the six point, the more uneven division of a given number of points is always the better one. For example, for five points, 4 and 1 is better than 3 and 2; for seven points, 5 and 2 is better than 4 and 3, but 6 and 1 is worst.

Table 11-3. Chances of Going Out from Various
Positions

Total needed	Points occupied	Ways to go out in one roll	Total needed	Points occupied	Ways to go out in one roll
12	6 and 6	4	7	5 and 2	19
				4 and 3	17
11	6 and 5	6		6 and 1	15
10	6 and 4	8	6	6 only	27
	5 and 5	6		5 and 1	23
				4 and 2	23
9	5 and 4	10		3 and 3	17
	6 and 3	10			
			5	5 only	31
8	5 and 3	14		4 and 1	29
	6 and 2	13		3 and 2	25
	4 and 4	11			
			4	4 only	34
				3 and 1	34
				2 and 2	26

The Doubling Cube

Much of the fascination of blackjack comes from the doubling cube. Wise doubling decisions require probability considerations. If your opponent doubles, you should accept if you have at least one chance in four of winning; winning $2 once and losing $2 three times is equivalent to losing $1 all four times. But if you have exactly one chance in four, the choice is not a complete toss-up. You are slightly better off by playing on because you will have possession of the doubling cube, which can be a real asset if the tide turns. On the other hand, if there is any possibility of losing a gammon or a backgammon, you should require slightly better odds for accepting the double.

When should you use the cube yourself? At the end of the game, the answer can be very simple. Suppose you are in a one-toss situation. It is your turn; if you go out you win, and if you don't go out, your opponent is sure to go out. In that case, you should double whenever you have better than a 50% chance of going out. If your opponent accepts, your expectation is doubled, and that's all there is to it.

But there are times when control of the doubling cube is so important that you should *not* double when you are a favorite to win. This can be the case even when you are odds-on to go out on your next roll and your opponent is not certain to go out on one roll if you fail! In the classic example, you control the cube and your two men are on points 5 and 2, while your opponent's men are on points 4 and 1. The analysis goes as follows:

Your winning probability includes the 19/36 (52.8%) probability of winning on your first roll, plus the probability of (17/36) × (7/36), or 9.2%, that you and your opponent will both fail on your first attempts.[3] This makes a total chance of 52.8% plus 9.2%, or 63%, that you will win; your expectation is thus $.62 minus $.38, or $.24 in a $1 game. If you double, you give away that extra 9.2% chance of winning the game, because as soon as you fail on your roll, the game will be over—your opponent will double, and you will have to refuse. (The odds will favor your opponent by 29 to 7, at that point.) With just the 52.8% chance of a one-roll win, your expectation is a mere $.11 even in the doubled ($2) game.

In some cases giving up the doubling cube can even turn a positive expectation into a negative one. For example, you have a man on your six point and a man on your one point, and your opponent's only man is on his six point. Your chance of winning on one roll is 5/12, and your overall chance of winning is 9/16, if you don't double. (You can work this out for yourself.) If you double, you sacrifice your second chance and are left with only the 5/12 chance of a one-roll win. Your double will have changed you from a favorite to an underdog and doubled the stakes in the bargain!

Backgammon has been studied for centuries, and there are many other recommendations that have been worked out on the basis of probabilities (either *a priori* or *a posteriori*). These include guidelines for doubling at earlier stages, as in a pure "running" game, on the basis of points needed to win, or number of turns required for going out. For more on the subject, read *The Backgammon Book*, by Jacoby and Crawford.[4]

CHAPTER 12

Insurance

You never encounter shady characters proposing strange bets, you don't go to casinos, your interest in sports ended when Marvelous Marv Throneberry retired, and at cards you haven't quite mastered the shuffle. But . . . you may still be gambling substantial sums each year—with your insurance agent, your stockbroker, and/or the people who sell you your Krugerrands. You also gamble with things more important than money—with your life or your health—whether you want to or not. In these last three chapters we'll see if you might be overlooking some chances to make better bets than you are making now.

Life Insurance

Every time you buy any kind of insurance, you are making a bet with the insurance company. You are betting that something bad will happen to you, and the company is betting that it won't happen. As in any other gamble, if you lose your bet, you lose your money. Fair enough; if you had won the bet, the company would have lost money.

Am I insulting your intelligence by making such an obvious statement? Perhaps, but you must understand that many insurance schemes obscure this basic point. When the life insurance salesman says, "The trouble with term insurance is that, if you live, you have nothing to show for it," he is pretending that insurance is something other than a bet. Just remember, if it isn't a bet, it isn't insurance. And if you can't lose, then it isn't a bet.

Another obvious fact is that the insurance company doesn't offer you the true odds on your bet: the company gets a healthy "house percentage." Otherwise, how could it pay its employees and finance those skyscrapers? But you willingly make the bet anyway because it protects you and your family from financial ruin—at least, it does if you are buying real insurance and not some gimmick.

There is no doubt that life insurance is a necessity for many people, and many have less than they should. Perhaps people feel that they can't afford as much as they really need. But if they realized how cheaply one can buy pure insurance, they would probably buy more.

Term Insurance

By "pure" insurance I mean *term* insurance—a simple bet with the insurance company. If you die during the term of the policy, the company pays off. If you live out the term, you've lost your bet; the company pays nothing, and nobody has any further obligation. You have "nothing left to show for it," but you got what you needed, insurance protection for a specified period, and you got it at a rock-bottom price.

The disadvantage of term insurance is that at the end of the term you might still need protection, and the company may not want to bet again. You may have become an unacceptable risk. You can avoid this possibility by buying *guaranteed renewable term insurance*. For a slightly higher initial premium, the company will commit itself, in a few years' time, to renewing a policy that they might otherwise want to drop. This additional commitment by the company naturally requires a higher premium when the policy is first issued.

Furthermore, it is understood that the policy will carry a still higher premium if and when it is actually renewed. At that time your increased age will increase the possibility that you will "win your bet"—that is, "cash in your chips." Table 12-1, which lists mortality rates, shows the true odds on life insurance for various age ranges on the assumption that the person is chosen at random from the white population. The mortality rate is significantly higher for the non-

Table 12-1. Mortality Rates in the United States

Age group	Number of deaths per 1,000 persons per year	
	White men	White women
Under 30	1.6	0.7
30 to 34	1.8	0.9
35 to 39	2.6	1.5
40 to 44	4.1	2.3
45 to 49	6.8	3.7
50 to 54	11.1	5.5
55 to 59	17.8	8.2

white population, but this difference is not a real factor in life insurance costs, for reasons to be discussed later.

The odds on people who are actually insured are often more favorable to the company because a physical examination is usually required. Some companies do sell insurance for which an exam is not required, but such insurance will obviously attract people who are such high risks that they cannot buy insurance otherwise. If you can pass an exam, you would be foolish to buy insurance that does not require one; you know that the company will have to charge higher rates to cover their higher risk.

Occupation as well as age can make a big difference in a person's risk. For that reason, companies charge higher rates to people in "high-risk classifications." We'll come back to this point later.

Neglecting correction factors, we can see from the table that a man aged thirty must pay $1.80 per year per $1,000 of five-year term insurance just to provide the company with enough money to pay the claims on all the thirty-to-thirty-four-year-old policyholders who die. If one of the surviving policyholders wants to renew his policy at age thirty-five, the company will then need $2.60 per year per $1,000 to meet the claims in his age group for the next five years.

The actual premiums are higher than this in order to cover the expenses of issuing the policy. But because administrative costs on a large policy are not much different from those on a small policy, the company should charge less per $1,000 of insurance on large policies. Some companies do this by paying dividends (rebates at the end of the year) that are larger per $1,000 of insurance on larger policies.

It is easy to shop around for the best rates on term policies because you know exactly what you are buying. But term insurance is not very popular because of a person's psychological resistance to paying higher rates as he grows older. The psychology is somewhat more favorable to the "decreasing term" policy, on which premiums remain constant but the death benefit decreases as the insured person grows older. Decreasing term makes sense for those whose savings increase and obligations decrease as they grow older (as children leave home and the mortgage is paid off).

Whole-life Policy

Insurance agents would rather sell a "whole life" policy, which has a constant annual premium as well as a constant face value. (The face value is also called the death benefit, although for a whole-life policy these expressions are not synonymous for reasons to be discussed in a moment.) With a risk that increases each year, the company can offer such a policy only by charging a premium that is far more than necessary to cover the initial risk (and incidentally provides a bigger commission for the agent). For example, a twenty-two-year-old woman bought a $20,000 whole-life policy at a premium of $340 per year. Even at age sixty she could buy term insurance more cheaply than that.

Cash Values

On the above-mentioned policy, only $12 to $15 of the annual premium covers the company's risk in the early years. The remaining part of the first-year premium goes into the agent's commission and the company's overhead and profit. In subsequent years, much of the premium goes toward building up a "cash value" for the policy. The cash value is money that actually belongs to the policyholder, and it is returned to her if she ever cancels the policy.

The cash value permits the premium to remain constant after the company's annual risk becomes greater than the premium, because by investing this money, the company makes earnings that can be applied toward covering this risk. The cash value also reduces the company's actual risk. When a company pays a "death benefit" of $20,000 on a policy with a cash value of $5,000, it is only paying out $15,000 of its own money. The other $5,000 belonged to the policyholder in the first place, and it would have had to be paid any time the policyholder wanted it.[1]

In many cases, you don't have to cancel your policy to get the cash value out of it. You can "borrow" your cash value as long as you pay interest on it; on older policies the interest rate is fixed at 5%. Some people think it is unfair to be required to pay interest on what is, after all, their own money. But it is quite fair. When you bought your policy, the premiums and cash values were fixed in anticipation of the company's ability to earn money by investing your cash value. If you take back your money, depriving the company of those earnings, you have to compensate the company by paying interest.

Because insurance companies are now able to earn much more than the modest 5% rate that they collect on the older policy "loans," they would like to persuade people to pay back those loans. They do this by warning that you lose some of your "protection" if you borrow on your policy. This is utter nonsense. That money will protect you just as well in your own savings account as it will in the insurance company's coffers. It is true that, if you die with a loan outstanding on your policy, your beneficiary will get less than the face value of the policy, but this has nothing to do with protection. Suppose that you owe $5,000 on a $20,000 policy, making the net benefit $15,000. Repaying the $5,000 just to bring the benefit up to $20,000 is as beneficial to you as buying a $5,000 insurance policy for $5,000.

You can't blame the insurance company for trying to get you to repay the loan, when you consider that they can earn a lot more than 5% by investing your money. But you can invest the money yourself and earn enough on it to cover the 5% interest and more. If you spend the money instead, you are still far ahead by paying 5% interest rather than the 15% or more that a commercial lender might charge.

If you take full advantage of your cash value by borrowing to the hilt, is whole life better to have than term insurance? It doesn't seem likely, because the agent's commission, which is based on the premium, will be larger for whole life. But if term is a better initial buy, it does not follow that you should cancel your present whole-life policy and switch to term. The commission comes mostly "off the top," that is, from the first year's premium. Once you have already bought whole life and paid the first premium, it is not usually wise to switch policies and pay another commission.

However, policies differ enormously, and there are also tax considerations, so only you can compute what is best for your own situation. To show you how to do this, let's make a cost analysis of the previously mentioned $20,000 policy, for which I have all the relevant figures. We'll figure the result for one year only.

Prudence and Zelma, identical twins, have identical policies, purchased eighteen years ago, with face value of $20,000 and a current cash value of $4,640 that is increasing at the rate of $300 per year. The policy's annual premium is $340, and it has paid a year-end dividend of $200 each year for several years. Each sister needs $4,300 to cover the costs of identical [what else?] emergencies. Zelma borrows the entire cash value of the policy. Prudence doesn't believe in borrowing [even if it's her own money], so she cashes in her policy and buys term insurance to replace it. [Naturally, she is prudent enough to determine that she is still insurable before she cancels her whole-life policy.]

Prudence needs only $15,000 in term insurance to maintain roughly the same protection that Zelma has; Zelma's policy will pay $20,000 minus $4,640 or $15,360, if she dies. Prudence can buy a $15,000 term policy for about $50, according to insurance company quotations for a woman aged forty who is a "preferred risk."[2] Now let's compare the two results for the year following the decisions to cancel or borrow:

Prudence	Net assets
1. cashes in policy, spends $4,300, pays $50 premium for term insurance, is left with:	$290
2. earns interest on $290 for one year, then pays tax on it, netting an additional:	$15
3. finishes the year with assets of:	$305

Zelma	
1. borrows $4,640 on policy, spends $4,300, pays premium of $340 to keep policy in force, leaving her:	0
2. at the end of the year receives $200 dividend and has a $300 cash value increase, giving her assets of:	$500
3. pays one year's interest on $4,640 at 5%:	−$232
4. claims tax deduction for $232 interest paid, gaining:	+$50
Finishes the year with net assets of:	$318

Without line 4, we see that Zelma's assets total less than her sister's; she has actually paid $37 more than Prudence for her insurance. But in the end, after the $50 tax saving, Zelma comes out ahead. [This wouldn't be the first time that a "tax subsidy" rewarded somebody for choosing the less economical of two alternatives.]

By following the same steps taken in working out this example, you can now decide whether to borrow on your own whole-life policy or to cash it when you need money. Taking into account all relevant factors—premiums for a replacement term policy, dividends, changes in cash value, loan interest, "time value" of cash in hand, and income tax deduction—you will probably find that the tax deduction tips the scales against cashing in your present policy.

Endowment Policies

A third type of policy is the "endowment" policy, a sort of souped-up whole-life policy with a cash value that increases so rapidly that at some point it equals the face value. At that point your true "death benefit" is nil; you collect the face value without the unpleasantness of dying. It sounds nice, doesn't it?

Unfortunately, if protection is what you want, you don't get much for your money. Throughout most of the policy's life, the potential payout consists mostly of your own money. It is a combined insurance and savings plan, with the drawback that you lose your insurance if you can't keep adding to your savings. Insurance agents like this type of policy, because larger premiums mean more commission for them [at your expense].

The appealing feature of the endowment is that you are guaranteed a certain amount of money—perhaps for your children's education—whether you live or die. But you can achieve the same goal by setting aside the amount that the endowment policy would cost, putting some of it into a decreasing term policy for the same initial face amount, and depositing the rest in a savings plan. Unless insurance rates have changed drastically by the time you read this, you will surely find that your combined savings and insurance will be equal to or greater than the initial amount of insurance. Your term policy will decrease less rapidly than your savings build up, and you will be well ahead at the time when you need the money. Your agent will argue that you need the discipline of "enforced savings"; but the large number of lapsed endowment policies testifies to the weakness of this argument.

Gimmicks

Finally, there are the life insurance "gimmicks"—insurance against specific ways of dying. It is hard to understand why your beneficiary would need more money if you died in an accident—a long illness is much more expensive—but the companies always offer an accidental death benefit as a "rider" on a policy at an extra cost of about $1 per $1,000 per year. That sounds cheap until you look at the accidental death statistics; the death rate from all accidents in the United States is about 0.5 per 1,000 per year. So the company pockets a hefty 50% on that rider, and what good is it? If you really need more insurance, use your available money to buy more coverage against all types of death instead of throwing the dice on a bet that gives the "house" a 50% edge.

The same argument applies to "travel insurance" policies

sold at airports. You pay about $1 per $30,000 for a single journey. If your chance of dying on that trip were anywhere near 1 in 30,000, you'd be taking the train, and so would everybody else.[3] The airlines would be out of business.

Another gimmick is "shark-bite insurance" inspired by the movie "Jaws." For a mere $25 you can buy $10,000 of insurance against death, dismemberment, or loss of sight caused by attacks from any one of twenty-one different threatening animals, including sharks, wolverines, and scorpions. How often do you think they pay off on that one?

High-risk Classifications

In buying all forms of insurance you pay rates that depend on the odds as seen by the company. Many factors affect these odds. Bartenders, policemen, and firemen must pay higher rates for life insurance; people living in areas with poor fire protection must pay more for fire insurance.

You may wonder whether it is fair that people who incur greater risks should pay higher rates, but fairness has little to do with it. It is a matter of free-market economics. Suppose that company A decides to charge appropriately higher rates to heavy smokers (up to 200% higher, depending on age; see table 14-1) while company B makes no distinction between smokers and nonsmokers. Company A can then substantially reduce their rates to everybody else, thereby gaining an advantage over Company B in competing for the business of nonsmokers. Company A will lose the business of the heavy smokers, but they will also lose the high risk involved, and therefore the loss of this business will not hurt their earnings.

More heavy smokers will sign up with company B, forcing this company to raise its rates to cover its increased risk and making B even less able to compete with A for the business of the nonsmoking majority. If all buyers of policies were to act in their own best interests, company B would eventually be insuring heavy smokers exclusively. At this point, company B's rates would equal the rates that company A charged to heavy smokers, all other factors being equal.

Thus the forces of competition operate as an incentive to

companies to classify risks whenever they can identify them. The moral is: If you are not in a high-risk category, look for a company that does classify the high risks so that you can get the lower rates that they must offer to people like you. [I'll bet you thought that the moral would be to quit smoking; but that's one of the morals of chapter 14.]

In spite of this powerful incentive to classify risks, there is at least one apparent high-risk group that is not classified: nonwhites, who as a group have a higher mortality rate than whites. Lest you think that this is unfair treatment of whites [possibly because of civil rights activity on behalf of minorities], consider what would happen if a company [say company A] were able and willing to charge higher rates to nonwhites.

Like the smokers in the previous discussion, nonwhites would take their business elsewhere. But events would then take a different course. Company A's remaining policyholders would not have lower average mortality rates than the policyholders who switched companies; there is no evidence that nonwhites *who buy insurance* are any less healthy than whites.[4] So company A would not be able to reduce its rates to whites and improve its competitive position. It would just lose part of its business.

For all kinds of insurance there may be hundreds of possible ways to put people into high-risk [or preferred-risk] classifications on the basis of "averages" like those we have been discussing. But a company has to make sure that any average really applies to its policyholders before it takes such a step. When a large number of people are involved, the company must ask itself: "If all of the people that we plan to put into the high-risk category were to take their business elsewhere, what would be the effect on our claims? Would we save enough to charge lower rates to other customers and thereby attract more business?"

Because decisions like this are so difficult, companies try to provide a way out of high-risk classifications whenever they can so that they can attract or keep the business of people who are not so great a risk as the "average" attributed to their classification. For example, one very high-risk category is that of the male teenaged driver. A teenager who has not yet had an accident or a traffic citation may argue that this is unfair. But even though he has driven safely so far, the company may still fear that he will succumb to the hazard (peculiar to the young male) of having to prove to his friends that he isn't a "wimp."

Nevertheless, many male teenagers consistently drive safely, and some companies have found a way to reward some of them—by giving a "good-student discount" to drivers who achieve high grades in school. This strategy is borne out by statistics, and the reason is not mysterious. A student who is getting good grades is not so likely to be someone who has to prove his manhood by taking a curve at ninety miles per hour.

Casualty Insurance

One basic consideration—that of cost versus benefit—applies to all kinds of insurance, including insurance against fire, theft, collision, earthquake . . . you name it. The policies come in a bewildering variety, but fortunately some policies, such as the standard "homeowners" policy, are now written in understandable English instead of the legal jargon that somehow combines ambiguity with redundancy.

After you have read your policy carefully, determined precisely what is and what is not covered, and attempted a comparison of premiums with those of other companies, the most important thing for you to inquire about is the "deductible" clause. This clause is the biggest moneysaver you can have in an insurance policy.

Consider the expense that an insurance company incurs in processing a small claim. Then remember that life insurance companies keep 50% of your premiums for such a simple thing as the "accidental death benefit" (which doesn't even require the paperwork of a separate payment) and you will realize that you get back a very small fraction of any premium that goes for covering small claims.

The only point in betting against a "house percentage" as high as 50% is to protect yourself against a financial disaster.

Table 12-2. Chances of Multiple Losses in a Given Time Period

Average number of losses in the period	Chance of x losses in that period				
	x = 0	x = 1	x = 2	x = 3	x = 4
0.05	.951	.048	.001	.00002	.0000002
0.1	.905	.090	.005	.00015	.000004
0.2	.819	.164	.016	.0011	.00006
0.3	.741	.222	.033	.0033	.00025
0.4	.670	.268	.054	.0072	.00072
0.5	.607	.303	.076	.0126	.00158
1.0	.368	.368	.184	.0613	.0153

A loss of a few hundred dollars is certainly unpleasant, but it is hardly any more disastrous than paying the policy's premiums in the first place. By taking the biggest deductible you can get, you can save a big portion of the premiums, put this money in the bank, and cover yourself against the smaller losses.

A deductible of $500 is well worth considering. This will cost you $500 any time your loss exceeds that amount. Clearly this will be a rare occurrence, for otherwise the company would not insure you. But what if you are unlucky and suffer several such losses? In that case you would have more than the deductible to worry about. The company would raise your rates and probably cancel your insurance.

Table 12-2 gives the probabilities for recurrences of major losses. You have to decide on the average number of losses to expect, on the basis of your own past experience as well as that of your neighbors. For example, suppose you decide that you would average one major loss in twenty years, and you want to know the probabilities for a ten-year period. On the line marked 0.5, you see that the probability of four losses would be .00158—about one in 630.[5]

Let's see how table 12-2 translates into a net gain or loss for you if you average 0.5 major losses in a ten-year period. If we neglect minor losses [under $500], we expect the deductible clause to cut your premiums by about twice the average expected loss,[6] or a total of $500 in the ten years. The resulting chances are:

Losses	Probability	Gain or loss
0	61%	gain $500
1	30%	break even
2	8%	lose $500
3	1%	lose $1,000
4	1/600	lose $1,500

It looks like a good bet. And it is even better than it looks here, because we have neglected the minor losses. Over a ten-year period, the deductible cannot fail to save you money on minor losses. The additional premium required to cover them will always be about twice as much as your expected losses. Furthermore, even if you are technically covered for those minor losses, you might decide not to report them, fearing that your rates would be raised. Why pay for coverage that you don't intend to use?

Conclusion

We have seen that insurance is a bet that you expect (and hope) to lose; the only purpose of the bet is to save you from catastrophe. You are not well served by a policy that dilutes this basic purpose, for it diverts money that could be used to increase your protection.

CHAPTER 13

Investments

Double your money in six years! Double your money in two years! Become a millionaire by investing a mere $2,000 a year in an IRA! How many times have you read pitches like that? How can you evaluate such claims? How can you compare the claimed results with the results you are now getting on your investments? How do you know whether you are investing or simply gambling at unfavorable odds? In this chapter we'll see how you might answer such questions. The first step is to look at the connection between the rate of growth of an investment and the value after a given number of years. This will allow us to put claims of large gains into perspective.

Growth Rates and Yields

A house that sold for $13,900 in 1951 was resold in 1976 for $112,900. If you were the buyer in 1951 and the seller in 1976, what was your annual rate of return on your investment before considering the expenses of owning the house?

The expression "annual rate of return" refers to the constant factor by which you would have to multiply each year to build the value up from its original value to its final value. For example, if you have an investment with a 5% growth rate [say a savings account that pays 5% compounded annually], the value is multiplied by 1.05 each year. After n years, the final value would be 1.05^n times the original value. In general, after growth at $r\%$ for n years, we have

$$[\text{Final value}]/[\text{original value}] = [1 + r/100]^n$$

So if we know the final and original values, we can take the nth root of their ratio, and the result will be the value of $1 + r/100$. For the house in question, the number of years is twenty-five, and the ratio of the final value to the original value is 1,129/139, or 8.12. The twenty-fifth root of 8.12 gives us the value of $1 + r/100$; it is 1.0874, as you can verify by working backwards. [You can take roots like this on any scientific calculator]. Therefore the value of $r/100$ is .0874, and the annual growth rate is 8.74%. Later we'll discuss what this means in terms of buying and selling property, considering the expenses involved in holding the property as well as in buying and selling it.

It sometimes helps to think about growth in terms of doubling time. At a steady growth rate, it will always take the same time to double your investment, no matter where you begin. For example, at 1% growth per year, your investment will double in seventy years. The time required is inversely proportional to the growth rate; at 2%, the doubling time is thirty-five years, and at x% it is very close to $70/x$ years, as long as x is less than ten. Shown below are some growth rates and the corresponding doubling times.

Growth rate [%]	41	19	12.2	9.1	7.2	5.9	5.1	4.4	3.9
Doubling time [years]	2	4	6	8	10	12	14	16	18

Retirement Income

Let us suppose that you have been successful in your investments. You are a single woman about to retire at age sixty-five, and through the years you have built your savings into a tidy nest egg. Now you want to use this nest egg to supplement your pension and social security.

Your life expectancy is seventeen more years, so you might consider investing the money and spending only the earnings on it, preserving the principal indefinitely to avoid the risk of outliving your money. But you can't take it with you; you might enjoy spending some of the principal before you go.

Let's look at the risk involved in dipping into the principal by using some hypothetical numbers. Say that you have $50,000 and you can get 8% per year, after taxes, with the safety you wish—that is, without buying X-rated bonds. This provides you with $4,000 per year indefinitely [that is, as long as the 8% rate persists]. How long would your income last if you decided to go for $5,000 per year by withdrawing from principal [assuming you could do that without sacrificing your rate of return on what is left]?

The answer is twenty years. If you withdrew $1,250 each quarter for eighty quarters, you would have $1,557 left at the start of the twenty-first year. You would have withdrawn only an extra $1,000 each year for twenty years, but the difference would amount to almost the entire $50,000. The difference is so large because your earnings would drop below $4,000 as soon as you made the first withdrawal from your principal, and your earnings would keep dropping every quarter as you made additional withdrawals. Because of the reduced earnings, your withdrawals from the principal would have to get bigger and bigger to maintain your $1,250 quarterly income. For example, because your first withdrawal included $250 from the principal, during the second quarter you would lose $5 in interest [2% of $250]. Your second withdrawal would therefore have to include $255 from the principal. The third withdrawal from the principal would be still larger, by 2% of $255. After eighty such geometrically increasing withdrawals, you would have taken $48,443 from the principal, leaving only $1,557.

In general, if the quarterly interest rate is $r\%$ and you want to maintain a constant quarterly income equal to W dollars more than your initial quarterly earnings, the sum of the first n withdrawals will be W times $[(1 + r/100)^n - 1] \times 100/r$. In our example, W is $250, r is 2, and n is 80, so the result is $[1.02^{80} - 1] \times 50 \times \$250$, which is $48,443.

Although, as a sixty-five-year-old woman, your average life expectancy is only seventeen years [or thirteen years if you are a sixty-five-year-old *man*], the risk of surviving to

Table 13-1. Chances of Surviving to Various Ages after Reaching Age 65

Age	70	75	80	85	90	95
Men	.83	.64	.41	.21	.08	.015
Women	.91	.79	.60	.39	.20	.06

the twenty-first year is great. Table 13-1 shows the probability of surviving to various specified ages if your age is sixty-five; you see that a woman has a 39% chance of living to the age of eighty-five. [A man is luckier; he has only a 21% chance of living that long.]

If you are willing to run the 6% risk of living to age ninety-five, you can use table 13-2 to see how to stretch your money that far. Given the numbers in the above example—$50,000 nest egg and 8% annual after-tax earnings—you can afford to spend only $4,410 per year, which is only $410 more than you get from taking the earnings and leaving the principal intact. And that is for an ideal situation; in practice you might have to sacrifice some of your earnings rate, or pay commission charges, if you want the flexibility to withdraw from principal every three months. But you can still use the table to figure what you can spend, on the basis of the net earnings that you have negotiated with your broker or banker.

The principal will last for the number of years shown in the second column if the amount shown in the last column is withdrawn annually in equal quarterly installments.

Annuities

Whenever you have a difficult monetary decision to make, somebody is always willing to take the burden off your shoulders—for a price. You can buy an annuity, which insures you against the misfortune of living too long. The company selling the annuity will pay the purchaser a specified amount of money at regular intervals as long as he or she lives. If the purchaser lives to be ninety-five, he or she has [probably] made a good deal. But the company isn't worried; for every person who lives to be ninety-five, there is someone who

dies at sixty-six or sixty-seven, forfeiting almost all of the price of the annuity.

Unfair? Of course not. On every bet there are winners and there are losers. The "house"—the company—only has to collect enough money to cover the average life expectancy plus expenses and profit. Even after allowing for profit, the company should be able to offer you a higher annual income than you can safely gain on the "do-it-yourself" plan calculated in table 13-2, because the annuitants who live "inherit" the money of the ones who die.

Taxes provide a powerful incentive for buying an annuity rather than trying to do it yourself. If you do it yourself, you must pay income tax each year on your investment earnings. On the other hand, (unless the tax laws are rewritten) you pay no taxes on a well-structured annuity until your total return exceeds the amount you originally invested, which could be ten years after your annuity begins. This has to save you a lot of money. (Please remember that I am not a tax expert, and I don't know your tax bracket; all I can do is tell you what to consider.)

Current tax laws give you an even bigger break if you begin to buy your annuity before you retire. An Individual Retirement Account (IRA) allows you to avoid paying income taxes on part of the income that you earn before retirement if you use it to buy shares in your IRA. The following comparison will show how big an advantage this is.

Morris and Boris are both in the 30% tax bracket, and each is putting aside a fixed amount each year for retirement. Morris puts his money into an IRA, and Boris invests his in other ways. If they both retire in ten years, what is the value of each one's annuity? To simplify, let's follow the growth of their assets year by year. Assume that each contributes to his investment (or IRA) at the beginning of each year, that each is credited with his investment (or IRA) earnings all at once at the end of the year, and that Boris pays taxes on his investment earnings at the end of each year.

To make a proper comparison, we must also take account of the taxes that Boris pays on his income before he invests. Assume that Morris and Boris have identical salaries and deductions and that they want to have the same after-tax income during their working years. If Morris earns $40,000 and puts $4,000 per year into an IRA, his taxable gross is only $36,000. Boris, whose taxable gross income is $40,000, pays $1,200 more tax than Morris, leaving him only $2,800 to invest. After one year, that $2,800 has earned only $280, and poor Boris has to pay another $84 tax on that. His $2,800 contribution for the second year brings his total to $5,796, while Morris has $8,400. Later years go:

	Boris	Morris
Start of year 3	$9,002	$13,240
Start of year 5	$20,029	$30,862
End of year 10	$41,394	$70,125

[In each case, I have assumed that the yearly investment is made at the beginning of the year.]

If both retire at this point, Boris will have a 41% smaller income than Morris on the basis of the net worth of their respective investments. However, Morris will have to pay taxes on his income, whereas Boris will probably be able to avoid paying any income tax on the return from his investment until he gets back the $41,394 that he already paid taxes on. Nevertheless, as you could have guessed, this will leave Morris comfortably ahead. Postponing payment of taxes has to be an advantage, even over a very small number of years.

Annuity Options

When considering the return from an annuity, you must pay attention to the conditions of payment. The above discussion applies to a single-person life annuity. If you die within a short time after buying this type of annuity, the company wins its bet, and that is the end of it. If you have others who are depending on you for support, you have two other options. The first will pay at the original rate as long as you and your spouse live, then continue to pay at a reduced rate after one of you dies, finally terminating when both of you have died. The second type guarantees a minimum number of payments to a designated beneficiary, no matter how soon you or your spouse may die, so that you can take care of somebody who may be depending on you for a limited number of years.

Obviously your initial annual income from either of these two types of annuity will be smaller than from the single-person type. But your net return still should be larger than what you could get by investing the money yourself and keeping the principal intact [see table 13-2]. If it isn't, then forget the annuity. You can always will your capital to a worthy charity or to your pet cat. [Notice that some charities will sell you an annuity, so that they will automatically inherit your capital upon your death. If you like the charity, check it out, but still consult the table to see if the return is worth it.]

Stocks and Bonds

Many people tend to think of stock purchases as gambles and bond purchases as conservative, safe investments. But buying bonds can be as much of a gamble as buying stocks. Even though you are not likely to lose all of your money on a bond, you can lose in several ways. Your investment can be eroded by inflation; you can take a loss if you have to sell the bond before its maturity date; or you can lose if the company [or city] goes bankrupt.

Bond Yields

The closest thing to 100% safety is achieved by investing in a bond that is nearing its maturity date. Let's see how to calculate the yield from such a bond, assuming that you will surely be able to hold it until it matures.

Say that you pay $8,000 [including commission] for a bond that will mature and pay $10,000 in five years and that the bond also pays interest at 4% per year. What is your annual rate of return on your investment? The 4% return on the $10,000 face value gives you $400, which is 5% of your actual investment. To that we have to add the average yield from the growth of your $8,000 to the maturity value of $10,000. We can compute that from the formula given at the beginning of this chapter; the ratio of the final value of $10,000 to the original value of $8,000 is equal to $1 + r/100$ raised to the fifth power, where r again is the percentage growth of your investment. The fifth root of this ratio is about 1.0456, so r is 4.56%, and your overall return is 9.56% per year on your so-called 4% bond. [If you are not able to reinvest your annual $400 interest at this rate, then the effective annual return over the five-year period is slightly smaller, but the difference is not very significant.]

Stocks

The safety of a bond is tempting, but we have seen that there is no safety in life. You can put your money into a savings account insured by the government of the richest nation on earth, but your funds will slowly "evaporate" from inflation. The same figures that we used for the doubling time of an investment also apply to the time required to slice an investment in half. At a 7% inflation rate, the money you hid in your mattress loses half of its value in ten years. And inflation is not likely to go away, although it may fluctuate in its severity.

For this reason, many people prefer to buy stocks or property with their money, figuring that these investments will go up in value as the price index rises. But this, too, is a gamble. While many people who disapprove of ordinary gambling may be investors, the uncertainty of the various markets leads many others to buy and sell often with the avowed purpose of gambling. There is a fine line between investing and gambling.

Let's go completely over to the gambling side of that line and see what's going on. Many people play the market the way others play the horses—betting on "hot tips," studying charts to see which stock may be ready to "make its move," etc. And as in horse betting, not only must you back a sound entry [stock], you must also outguess the other bettors [excuse me, I mean investors].

If you are constantly switching from one stock to another, guessing is just what you are doing. If you think you know why a stock, or the whole market, rises or falls in the short term, you are just kidding yourself. If you doubt this, read the expert analysts' explanation of market movements: ''The market was reacting to fears of higher interest rates, the crisis in Upper Volta, Cyprus, Sri Lanka . . . unemployment.'' You name it, they'll give it as a reason. The problems had been around for months or years, and then the market suddenly decided to react to them on one particular Tuesday. Sure.

Maybe you can outguess the market (some of the time), and you might enjoy the challenge. You still should be aware of the big house percentage you are paying when you gamble in this way. Brokers' commissions may vary, but unless you deal in really large amounts, the total commission on buying and selling averages about 6% of the total cost of your shares. In itself, that would be a stiff enough percentage to try to beat, but the effective percentage is much higher because of the way in which this gambling is done.

Suppose you buy a stock selling at 30. You might well decide to sell it if it rises to 40 or if it falls to 20. In that case, on a hundred shares you stand to win or lose $1,000 before commissions. But the total commission is about $180, so you actually win only $820 if you are right, and you lose $1,180 if you are wrong. This means that the ''house edge'' is 18%; at that rate, you might as well be betting on the ponies.

Many gamblers think that they can beat this huge house percentage by following charts and trying to extrapolate past ''cycles'' to predict future prices. It is easy to read cycles into a record of past performance, but the future is another matter. Look again at the ''random walk'' in figure 2-3 (chapter 2). It looks a lot like a stock market chart, doesn't it? You can see cycles, and you can see things that look like the market analysts' ''resistance levels,'' but you know that the coin generating the walk knows nothing about all of this. What reason is there to believe that the market is any more predictable than this coin if the chart is all you have to go on?

But, you say, I know this fellow who got rich by taking advantage of cycles in wheat futures. Maybe you do, but I knew a fellow who found a ''sure-fire'' cycle (one that had repeated for seven straight years]. He discovered that it failed when he backed it heavily. He lost more than his money; he committed suicide.

There is no need to go into all the other ways that speculators find to try to predict the unpredictable. In years when the market is steadily rising, these traders look like geniuses; they make profits on every deal. Before joining their ranks, ask yourself if you will make more by frequent dealing than you would by buying sound stocks and staying with them. Sooner or later the "greater fool theory" must fail. [This theory, popular in the 1960s, says, "No matter what ridiculously high price I pay for a stock, a greater fool will pay more for it later."]

The bottom line is this: The "house edge" is just as tough to beat in the stock market as it is in the horse races.

Options: Puts, Calls, and Straddles

If you really want to gamble in stocks, the way to do it with minimum capital is to buy options, which give you much more action for your money. I do not recommend that you run out and buy some options, but they do have certain advantages for the gambler, and they also can be useful to the investor.

A "call" is an option giving you the right to buy a specified amount of stock at a fixed price at any time until the call expires. For example, on January 28, 1975, you could have bought a three-month call on 3-M Corporation, entitling you to buy 100 shares of common stock at $45 per share during the following three months. The call would have cost you $412.50 plus $25 commission. On that same date, you could have bought a six-month call for $550 plus commission, or you could have bought 100 shares of the stock itself for $4,575 plus commission.

If you buy the option instead of the stock, you need less capital, and you can never lose more than the cost of the option. On the other hand, you make no profit until the stock price rises enough to cover the cost of the option. Buying the option has one big advantage for the gambler: if he bought the stock and it suddenly dived in price, he might have to sell it to limit his loss; but having bought a call, he has a chance that the stock will recover before his call expires. On the other hand, the time limit is a disadvantage; if the stock goes nowhere before your call expires, you lose, but if you had the stock itself, you could hold on to it and hope for a later improvement.

You can also buy a "put." The seller of a put sells you the right, for a limited time, to sell a number of shares of a given stock to him at a specified price. You can buy a put even if you don't own the stock. If the stock goes down, you can then buy it and make a profit by exercising your put.

The put allows you to bet on a decline in price even if you have no stock to sell. You can do the same thing by "selling short," which is borrowing a stock and then selling it, but selling short can be very risky. Eventually you must buy the borrowed stock and return it to the lender. If the stock starts to rise in price, you have a tough decision to make; you could lose a bundle if you "hang on."

Yet another way to gamble is to buy a "straddle," which is a put and a call on the same stock. This is a bet that the stock will move a lot, one way or the other. If the price holds steady, you lose.

Buying options looks attractive because with a limited risk you can bet on either a rise or a fall in price, and the cost allows you to make several bets for the price of a single outright purchase of stock. But you can be sure that the price of each option is set by people who know at least as much about the stock's future prospects as you do. If buying options were a good way to get rich, it would mean that the sellers always set their prices too low. Fat chance.

The sellers appear to know what they are doing, and the prices that they set tell us something about random fluctuations. For a given stock, a six-month option to buy at the current market price costs you about 40% more than a three-month option. If stock prices follow a "random walk" [chapter 2], then the probabilities on the future price of any stock must follow a normal distribution, in which the mean is the current price and the standard deviation is proportional to the square root of the number of "trials"—that is, to the elapsed time. So if you double the time, you multiply the standard deviation by about 1.4, and a six-month option must be worth 1.4 times the value of a three-month option.

While options are a prime vehicle for gambling, they can also be used in special investing situations. Let us suppose that you have bought a stock intending to hold it for the long run, but it suddenly rises in price. You believe that your stock is now overpriced, so you would like to sell it and protect your profit. But if you sell too soon, your profit will be taxed as a short-term gain. To avoid this, you buy a put, allowing you to sell the stock later at the present high price. This is profitable if the cost of the put is significantly smaller than the amount of tax you save by postponing the sale. If the stock price stays up, you have "wasted" the price of the put, but you are still better off than you would have been by selling the stock earlier. In this case, buying the put is a way to *avoid* gambling—to lock in most of your profit.

Advantages of Investing in Stocks

Investing in stocks, as opposed to gambling, has definite advantages over savings certificates or bonds. Although stocks are not the reliable "hedge" against inflation that they used to be, the stock investor gains in two ways: [1] If the stock price rises, he pays no tax on that gain until he sells the stock. [2] When he does sell the stock, he pays tax on his profit at the low "capital gains" rate [presently only 40% of what he would pay on "ordinary" income].

To see the effect of these advantages, let's return to Boris and Morris, who have each just inherited $1,000 from their Uncle Horace. Boris buys a savings certificate that pays 10% annual interest for five years. Morris buys a stock that pays no dividends but goes up in price at an average rate of 10% per year over those five years. If they are both in the 30% tax bracket, how does each fare?

His annual income tax reduces Boris's net rate of return to 7%. At the end of five years, he has $1,402.55 after taxes [$1.07^5$ times $1,000]. Morris has $1,610.51 before taxes [$1.1^5$ times $1,000], and he is left with $1,537.25 after paying the capital gains tax of $73.26 [12% of his earnings]. Even if

Morris had to pay tax at the full 30% rate, he would end up with $1,427.36, having gained about $25 solely through the postponement of his tax payments.

Obviously, there was no guarantee that Morris's stock would rise at any particular rate, but this example shows how large an "edge" you have when you buy a good stock. The combined effect of delaying a tax payment and then paying at the reduced capital gains rate is so potent that Morris needed only an average return of about 7.8% per year to do as well as Boris did at 10%.

For this reason it is hard to sympathize with the fellow who complains that he is "locked in" to a stock—meaning that he can't afford to sell it because he would then, finally, have to pay a modest tax on the considerable profit coming to him. He has already had a hefty tax break, but he wants to pay no tax at all. Such people are sometimes wiped out without ever benefiting from their gains. Remember the old Wall Street adage: "Bulls get a little, bears a little, but hogs get nothing."

Property

People who are concerned about inflation (and who isn't?) have traditionally bought stocks to protect themselves. The idea was that, in the long run, stock prices would have to rise as money loses its value, and therefore the investor who was willing to ignore short-term fluctuations could protect his savings by buying sound stocks.

But the "long run" has become very long indeed. On December 31, 1969, the Dow-Jones Industrial Average (of prices of thirty "blue-chip" stocks) stood at 800.36, and Standard & Poor's 500-stock average was 92.06. Fourteen years later, these averages had both increased by about 70%, but the consumer price index had almost tripled.

There are theories to explain this relatively poor performance of stock prices, but they do not concern us here. By now you should be convinced that you can't predict the future and that publicly trying to do it is a good way to get egg on your face. (In 1974 noted economist Dr. Milton Friedman said that oil prices could not rise above $10 a barrel and would probably decline in the succeeding few years.] The point is that people are continually searching for things to buy that will give them the inflation protection that stocks do not seem to be providing. The search has taken them to real estate, stamps, coins, works of art, rare books, diamonds, antiques, gold, silver, platinum—the list could go on and on. The argument in favor of investing in the property in question is always the same; there is a limited supply of that particular item and an increasing money supply, so the cash value of such an "investment" must increase. This argument is superficially attractive, but it overlooks several important factors:

The Value of a Rarity

How do you determine the "value" of a rarity, such as a rare stamp or an original work of art? We are discussing investing, so let's forget that overworked word "priceless;" if you own something and have to sell it to raise cash, its value to you at that moment is only what someone is willing to pay you for it. Although the price index and the general money supply may have doubled since you bought a painting, you have no assurance of finding a buyer who is willing to pay twice what you paid. You are forced to deal with a minute fraction of the population in which there can be great fluctuations, up or down, in the level of interest in any particular item.

You may say that a great work of art has "universal" appeal. However, if the cash value of a work were solely determined by its esthetic appeal, then a clever forgery would be worth as much as the original because nobody has the X-ray vision necessary to tell them apart.

Past Price Performance

One guide to cash value is the actual past performance of the price of a rarity, which at least tells us what its value was. At first glance, a study of past prices seems to bear out the theory that rarities are good investments. But often the prices you see are just the prices that dealers in these items choose to parade before your eyes.

A newspaper ad asks, "How many investments can show an annual increase in value of 27%?" It goes on to say, "A random selection of twenty-four rare stamps shows an average annual compound growth rate of 27.2% over the thirteen years 1966–1979 [catalogue value]." The statement may be perfectly true, but the term "random" is suspect. Who made the random choice, and how was it done? Remember too that they were free to choose whatever set of years looked best. Finally, consider that the growth rate cited by ads like these tends to feed on itself; it depends on a growth of popularity that in turn is generated by the growth rate itself [the "greater fool" theory again].

Who knows how long this sort of positive feedback can continue? The British Rail Pension Funds spent £28 million on an art collection, and they planned to spend at least £12 million more, according to the *Manchester Guardian*. What happens to prices in the art world when people who run such funds decide that this is too risky a way to invest pensioners' money?

Rising prices of precious metals have often made coins look like an excellent investment. After the United States stopped making coins from silver, a boom developed in prices of pre-1965 silver coins. If you had paid $1,750 for an uncirculated 1896-S [San Francisco mint] quarter in 1973, you would have been quite pleased with yourself in 1980 when the price had risen to $6,000. But in 1984, when the price hit $2,750, you might have wondered why you hung onto that "investment." The net increase from $1,750 to $2,750 represented a little better than 4% annual growth—far less than savings accounts were paying. During the same eleven years, there were other coins that did much better; an uncirculated 1901-S quarter went from $2,300 to $8,250. Other coins have done much worse. If you had bought an uncirculated 1950-D [Denver mint] nickel in 1951 at the going price of $25, you could sell it today for a cool $6. How are you to predict which coins will perform? Maybe you would be better off buying comic books, Coca-Cola signs, or toys.[1]

Cost of Investing

A third factor to consider is the cost of investing, including the dealer's commissions and the cost of caring for your properties. "Diamonds are forever," they say; you almost have to keep them forever to overcome the dealer's markup. [Try selling a diamond you have just bought, and you'll see what I mean.] Look again at that 27% annual growth quoted for rare stamps. Suppose you are lucky enough to buy a stamp that does that well, but then you have to raise money, say, three years after you bought it. At 27%, compounded annually, the retail price will have risen by 105% in three years. If you bought the stamp for $100, it would retail at $205 when you sell it. But you might get only 60% of the retail price from a dealer for it. The result, $123, works out to a modest annual gain of 7%. To get even that much, you had to take good care of that stamp.

It is often claimed that buying a home is the best investment of all because real-estate prices seem to rise every year. But should you buy a bigger home than you need, not because you enjoy rattling around in it, but because it would be a good investment? To assess this sort of purchase strictly as an investment, you must consider all the expenses of ownership—extra taxes, extra repairs, extra utility bills, cleaning, painting, etc. For the house mentioned at the beginning of this chapter, the 8.74% annual growth in value hardly seems to cover expenses, leaving you no return at all on your "investment."

If you were using the house, it wouldn't matter. You should expect to pay something for a place to live. But if you were foolish enough to buy a bigger house than you really wanted to live in, just as a place to invest additional money, you made a very bad decision. Obviously, this conclusion holds only for the particular numbers given in this example, which may or may not indicate future trends accurately. But the overall increase in price does look impressive at first sight, doesn't it?

In home buying, as in other investments, you still have to consider that prices can go down as well as up. Many people have bought several homes on marginal financing, just as investments. If a downturn in the economy forces these people to sell, prices could tumble. There are no ''sure things'' in which to invest.

Phony Prices

A fourth consideration that might surprise you is that the prices you read for some rarities are not genuine sale prices at all, even though a ''sale'' has been announced in the newspapers. Leading London auctioneers Sotheby's and Christie's have admitted that they take bids ''from the chandelier''—that is, imaginary bids. They, as well as other auctioneers, usually have a minimum price, below which an object will not be sold. But they don't tell that to anybody when they are auctioning the item. Instead, they take phony bids ''from the chandelier'' until the minimum price has been reached. If the minimum is not reached, they go through with the charade and announce a ''sale'' for, say £1,000, when no sale actually occurred because the minimum was £1,100. According to news reports, 20% to 30% of the Impressionist paintings auctioned in recent years were not actually sold, although a sale was announced and a ''sale price'' was reported.

Summary

In this chapter I have tried to show how to evaluate growth rates and returns on investments, so you can decide for yourself where to put your money. I hope you will forgive me if it appeared too pessimistic, but somebody has to point out the negative side of various ways of investing. The promoters aren't about to do it. Don't be dazzled by huge increases in prices; this is a natural effect of compounding a growth rate, even a modest rate. Remember that if you had bought one acre of land in the middle of Manhattan in 1850, today you would be dead.

It makes sense to buy stamps or coins if you get pleasure from a collection, and any profit you make is a bonus that you aren't counting on. But if you act on a tip or an ad to buy something you are unfamiliar with, and then put it in a vault hoping it will increase in value, you are taking a wild gamble. Furthermore, you are betting against people who know a lot more about that particular market than you do. If you must invest in this way, make a hobby of it; then you will at least have some pleasure to show for it. Eventually you could become enough of an expert yourself to make some money, but don't rely on it.

The gambles discussed in this chapter are more respectable than betting on the horses, and many of them are unavoidable. But they are gambles just the same. As in betting on horses, you must not only pick a winner, but pick an underpriced winner to come out ahead. But here the choice is much tougher because you never know when the "race" is over. It ends when you have had enough. You are the winner if the merits of your "horse" are more apparent when you sell than they were when you bought.

What do you fancy for the twenty-first century—antique electronic calculators, railroad shares, copper coins, smurfs? Go ahead and try to guess, if it gives you a thrill. But don't expect to beat the "house"—the dealers who get their percentage regardless. If you break even, you'll have done better than most of us.

CHAPTER 14

You Bet Your Life

When you gamble, it is not only with money or possessions. Often you bet your life or your health. Sometimes this is done for a noble cause, but more frequently it is for a trivial reason. For example, you may drive faster because you are late for the theatre, or you may fool around with a dangerous substance because you don't want to be a "party pooper."

Maybe you don't care about the risks involved in these activities, and learning about the odds won't make any difference. But there is more to this than cold figures; all the figures presented here represent tragedies that could be prevented. Why don't we try to avoid these tragedies? Partly because we shut the possibilities out of our minds.

We don't see accident victims in the flesh. We don't see people in the cancer wards, still puffing on the smoke that is killing them. Or if we do see them, we think of them as old people whose time has come instead of as people who should be in the prime of life and who are leaving small children for someone else to rear. And we certainly don't see victims of a nuclear holocaust; if we ever were to see them, it would be far too late to think about how it could have been prevented.

Actual and Perceived Dangers

The general public has a very distorted view of the relative hazards in various activities. As a result, serious problems can be overlooked while we waste time and money on less important matters. Before reading on, test yourself. How many annual deaths would you say occur in the United States

Nancy A. Burgard

as a result of each of the following: alcohol; commercial aviation; diagnostic X rays; handguns; motor vehicles; motorcycles; nuclear power; and tobacco? Compare your answers with the data and calculations given in this chapter.

The dangers that attract public attention are those that make headlines. When people have been asked to estimate the frequencies of death from various causes, the most overestimated categories are those involving accidents, pregnancy [including childbirth and abortion], tornadoes, floods, fire, and homicide. The most underestimated categories include deaths from diseases such as diabetes, stroke, tuberculosis, asthma, emphysema, and stomach cancer [although cancer in general is overestimated].[1]

These patterns in surveys are closely related to newspaper coverage. There are three times as many articles about homicide as about all diseases combined, although diseases take a hundred times as many lives as homicides.[2]

When people are asked to estimate the risks of death from various activities and technologies, the same faulty perception shows up. The familiar is never seen as threatening, and what seems to be under their control seems less threatening than the sort of technology that gives them no choice [for example, nuclear power].

If you engage in a dangerous activity and do not experience its harmful effects, you become convinced that the activity is relatively benign. If you drive fast and tailgate other drivers and you get away with it, then you must be a safe driver, and you certainly don't need a seat belt. [Scenes of accident victims on the eleven o'clock news merely show that accidents happen to other people.] Similarly, if you have smoked for twenty years and are still alive, then smoking can't be as bad as the surgeon general says it is. You can quit any time you want to—just as soon as your doctor orders you to—and everything will be OK. Or so you think.

A survey of three different groups of people showed that each group vastly underestimated smoking and consuming alcohol as activities that cause death. Their estimates were too low by factors of ten to twenty! They came closer [although still too low] on motor vehicles. In contrast, people overestimated the deaths from commercial aviation. Your probability of being killed on any given commercial airline flight is roughly one in a million; your chance of being killed during a transcontinental auto trip is about 1 in 8,000. Which of these activities would you be more apprehensive about?

Let us now examine some activities and hazards in more detail. We'll begin with the number-one killer.

Tobacco

Tobacco smoke, including pipe, cigar, and cigarette smoke, contains thousands of chemical compounds, many of them known to be toxic. Therefore it should be no surprise that smoking can cause a variety of ailments. It would take a medical encyclopedia to describe them all, from chronic bronchitis, cancer, heart disease, and strokes to ulcers [which are impossible to cure unless the patient quits smoking] and wrinkles [no kidding].

Overall Mortality

In 1960, Dr. E. C. Hammond conducted a survey of smoking habits of 447,196 men. These men were all living (and none was seriously ill) on July 1, 1960. Almost all (about 98.9%) of them were traced for the next five years, and it was found that 39,178 died during that period. Table 14-1 shows the relative numbers of deaths in various groups, classified according to age and smoking habits.

The number of men sampled in each category was around 10,000, hence the results are statistically significant. (A 4% probability, for 10,000 men, would give 400 deaths with a standard deviation of 20, or 0.2%; see chapter 2.) The uniformity of the trends in the numbers confirms that random fluctuations must be considerably smaller than the differences between the numbers.

The observed death rates were used to compute the numbers of survivors expected at each age, if one started with 1,000 men at age twenty-five in each category. These numbers are also shown in table 14-1. You can work them out for yourself by starting at the top. For example, taking away 1.2% of the original 1,000 heavy smokers would leave 988 at age thirty; taking away 1.5% of those 988 would leave 973 at age thirty-five, and taking away 2.3% of those 973 would leave 951 at age forty.

These figures were used to compute the average life expectancy for each group. The twenty-five-year-old, forty cigarettes-per-day smoker was found to have a remaining life expectancy of 40.3 years, or 8.3 years less than that of a nonsmoker of the same age. The twenty-five-year-old may not care what happens in forty years, but the effect doesn't wait for forty years to show up. Much of the reduction in this average life expectancy results from people who die in the prime of life. The overall death rate of smokers exceeds that of nonsmokers in each age group from age twenty-five on, and the rate for heavy smokers is *triple* the rate for nonsmokers between the ages of forty and fifty.

Notice the parallel here between the numbers for nonsmokers and the numbers for heavy smokers who are *ten years younger*. If you issued ten-year term life insurance pol-

Table 14-1. Percentage of Men Dying in Five Years, and Number of Survivors, Classified by Amount of Smoking

| | Percentage of Deaths | | | | Number of Survivors | | | |
| | *Number of Cigarettes per Day* | | | | *Number of Cigarettes per Day* | | | |
Age	Zero	1–9	10–39	40+	Zero	1–9	10–39	40+
25	0.6	0.9	0.9	1.2	1,000	1,000	1,000	1,000
30	0.7	1.0	1.0	1.5	994	991	991	988
35	0.9	1.5	1.6	2.3	987	981	981	973
40	1.4	2.5	2.7	4.3	978	966	965	951
45	2.1	3.8	4.6	5.9	964	942	939	910
50	3.7	5.2	7.3	9.2	944	906	896	856
55	5.9	9.4	10.5	13.6	909	859	831	777
60	9.1	13.5	16.4	19.5	855	778	744	671
65	14.2	22.1	24.8	25.9	777	673	622	540
70	21.6	30.9	32.1	35.8	667	524	468	400

Numbers in the first four columns give the percentage of persons in each group who will die during the next five years. Numbers in the next four columns give the number expected to survive to the given age out of 1,000 men at age twenty-five.

SOURCE: Numbers in the last four columns are from E. C. Hammond, *Journal of the National Cancer Institute*, 43 [1969], 951–962. Reprinted in *Dangers of Smoking, Benefits of Quitting*, rev. ed. [American Cancer Society, 1980].

icies to forty-five-year-old nonsmoker Joe Schultz and to his brother Moe, a thirty-five-year-old heavy smoker, you would be more likely to pay off on young Moe [assuming that Moe continues to smoke and Joe does not take leave of his senses]. The table shows that the probability of dying during the next ten years is about 6.5% [63/973] for young Moe and about 5.7% [55/964] for older brother Joe.

To put it another way, if you are a twenty-five-year-old nonsmoking male, the odds are 7 to 2 in favor of your reaching the age of sixty-five. If you smoke one pack of cigarettes a day, the odds are only 3 to 2. If you smoke two packs a day, you have barely more than an even chance to collect social security at age sixty-five. The table shows that even your chance of reaching the ripe old age of thirty is noticeably reduced by smoking. Among 1 million heavy smokers aged twenty-five, there will be 6,000 more deaths before age thirty than there will be in an equal number of twenty-five-year-old nonsmokers. Considering the population as a whole, there are about 300,000 premature deaths among smokers each year.

If you had only these statistics to go on, you could rightly suspect that something other than smoking could be the culprit. Perhaps smokers simply have more hazardous lifestyles, poorer health care, or more dangerous occupations. So let us go beyond the overall statistics to see how these deaths occur.

Respiratory Illness

Your lungs are protected by tiny hairs, called cilia, which brush out foreign matter. Inhaled smoke destroys the cilia, leading to an increase in production of mucus, coughing, and eventually chronic bronchitis. Every stage of this process can be monitored in smokers. Before any illness is apparent, lung function can be measured scientifically and correlated with smoking habits. Loss of lung function has been observed in teenagers who have smoked for as little as one year.

Loss of the lungs' ability to clear themselves leaves the victim defenseless against air pollutants and respiratory infections. A study of factory workers showed that smokers became ill 3.5 times as often as nonsmokers; this and other studies showing similar results are reported in the Cancer Society booklet cited in table 14-1. Some of these illnesses could account for the fact that the higher mortality rates in table 14-1 show up even in the younger age groups.

Besides putting its victims in a position to die of various diseases at an early age, chronic bronchitis fosters the development of emphysema, a fatal disease that causes great suffering. *Ninety-eight percent of emphysema patients have been smokers,* according to the March 1979 newsletter of Action on Smoking and Health [ASH], Washington D.C.

Overall, deaths from chronic obstructive lung disease [chronic bronchitis and emphysema] rose from 2,000 per year in 1945 to 23,000 per year in 1977. The above facts show it to be more than a mere coincidence that a great increase in smoking preceded this rise.

Cancer

You already know that cancer is something to be avoided, and everyone outside the tobacco industry knows it is linked to smoking. So let's just give the probabilities and see how some of the conclusions are reached.

Cancer of the lung has been correlated to smoking in minute detail. Incidence of lung cancer increases with the number of cigarettes smoked. It is greater for those who begin to smoke at an earlier age, and it is smaller for ex-smokers than for those who continue to smoke. Men who started to smoke before age fifteen have a death rate nearly four times as high as those who began after age twenty-five.

Women, who are exposed to the same air pollution as men, had much lower lung cancer rates when few women smoked. But the lung cancer death rate in U.S. women rose by 1,000% between 1930 and 1980; it became the fifth leading cause of death from cancer in U.S. women in 1964, and it rose to second place in 1977. It will probably be in first place when you read this; the percentage of smokers among teen-aged girls nearly doubled [from 8.4% to 15.3%] between 1968 and 1974.

In the March 1971 issue of *American Scientist*, Dr. Alton Ochsner gave detailed figures relating lung cancer to tobacco use in the United States. The incidence of lung cancer, per 100,000 persons, was:

- Nonsmokers   3.4
- Cigar smokers   11.4
- Pipe smokers   28.4
- "Light" cigarette smokers   51.4
- "Moderate" cigarette smokers   59.3
- "Heavy" cigarette smokers   143.9
- "Very heavy" cigarette smokers   217.3

"Light" cigarette smoker means someone who smokes less than half a pack a day, "moderate," one-half to one pack a day, "heavy," one to two packs per day, and "very heavy" you can guess. A heavy smoker has over sixty times the risk of a nonsmoker. It is difficult to imagine how the above facts, considered as a whole, could be correlated with any other variable in such a way that smoking could be exonerated.

Similar numbers are found worldwide. Some results have been compiled by T. Hirayama in the book *Lung Cancer 1982*.[3] In one study, 265,118 healthy adults in Japan were interviewed in connection with the 1965 census, and their records were checked regularly thereafter. In the first thirteen years, there were 1,244 lung cancer deaths; this worked out to a mortality rate of 20.7 for nonsmokers, 177.6 for very heavy smokers, and intermediate rates for less heavy smokers. [Similar results were found in smaller-scale studies in India, China, and the Philippines.] The rate for very heavy smokers is about nine times the rate for nonsmokers—not quite so high a ratio as in Ochsner's figures, because the rates for Japanese nonsmokers appear to be higher. This higher rate for nonsmokers could be a result of "passive smoking" [discussed below] because of the more crowded conditions and the higher percentage of smokers in Japan [73% of adult males smoke, compared to about 40% in the United States].

The tobacco industry "explains" higher lung cancer rates for smokers by saying that a genetic disposition toward smoking might be coupled with a genetic susceptibility to lung cancer. Ingenious, but it doesn't explain the smoking beagles. In 1970, ninety-seven healthy beagles were divided into several groups—a nonsmoking control group, plus groups that were forced to smoke cigarettes. After 875 days, forty dogs were killed and examined. All twelve of the dogs that smoked the dog-equivalent of two packs a day had lung tumors, but only two of the eight nonsmoking dogs had tumors. Five of the ten one-pack-a-day dogs had tumors, as did four of the ten filter-tipped cigarette smokers. The researchers said that the changes observed in the lung tissue were "the same in the beagle as in man."

Many other forms of cancer are related to tobacco use. A brief listing follows.

Cancer of the bladder: 84% of the victims are smokers. It has been induced in mice by application of tobacco to the oral cavity. Cancer develops in the bladder because cigarette smoking interferes with the excretion of certain carcinogens in the urine. In laboratory tests, levels of these carcinogens in the bladder have been found to fall when subjects stop smoking.

Cancer of the esophagus: incidence in smokers is two to nine times the incidence of nonsmokers. The rate depends on the amount of smoking and on the consumption of alcohol, which apparently facilitates the penetration of cancer-causing chemicals from tobacco into the body.

Cancer of the larynx: autopsies of smokers have shown that 100% of one-pack-a-day smokers had abnormal (precancerous) cells in the larynx; only 25% of nonsmokers have such cells. People who had quit smoking had abnormal cells that were *disappearing* and being replaced by normal cells.

Cancer of the lips, tongue, and mouth: 90% of victims use tobacco—either smoking it, chewing it, or putting "just a little pinch between the cheek and gums."

Cancer of the pancreas: rate is five times as great for smokers as for nonsmokers.

Sudden Death

Smoking can lead to sudden death in several ways. It causes directly observable changes in the circulatory system, which often lead to fatal heart attacks and strokes even among relatively young people. On the other hand, stopping smoking leads to a reduction in risk after only one year. Observation of 4,000 men over a period of eight years showed that men who smoked twenty or more cigarettes per day had three times as much chance as nonsmokers of developing coronary heart disease and that this extra risk was eliminated for those who stopped smoking. Sudden deaths from coronary heart disease before the age of fifty are sixteen times as frequent in smokers of twenty or more cigarettes per day as in nonsmokers; in other words, a smoker's heart attack is more likely to be fatal, and for good reason.

The mechanism linking tobacco to these effects is no mystery. Autopsies of 2,000 men who died from all causes showed that the walls of the blood vessels in all subjects tended to thicken with age, but that thickening was considerably greater in smokers than in nonsmokers. Furthermore, the amount of thickening increased with the number of cigarettes smoked. [This was a "blind" study; the scientists analyzing the blood vessels did not know the smoking habits of the subjects; therefore they could not be biased in their judgments of thickening.] In another study, fibrous thickenings in the walls of small blood vessels in the heart were found in 91% of heavy smokers, in 48% of light smokers, and in none of those who had never smoked.

While the blood vessels are losing their ability to carry blood, the blood itself is losing the ability to carry oxygen. Carbon monoxide [CO] in smoke combines with hemoglobin to form carboxyhemoglobin [COHb], reducing the amount of hemoglobin available to carry oxygen. Levels of COHb in smokers are several times those in nonsmokers and high enough to impair eyesight and coordination as well as heart function. [On the island of Sark, where there are no autos, the CO level in the blood of nonsmoking inhabitants is about 0.7%. In 100 nonsmoking Londoners, the CO level averaged 1.12%; in Londoners who smoke, the level was found to be 5.5%.[4] So smoking has a far greater effect than big-city pollution in raising CO levels in the blood.]

Because of this impairment, a male airline pilot who smokes twenty cigarettes per day has a risk of sudden death that is 2.8 times that of a nonsmoking male pilot of the same age. The same increased risk is present when smokers are driving autos. A study of 105,000 policyholders by the State Mutual Life Assurance Company of America showed that smokers have 2.6 times as many fatal accidents as nonsmokers. The concentration of smoke in the confined space of a car makes the CO problem even more acute than in a plane. [Attending to smoking materials instead of the road may also affect the accident rate.] Levels of CO as high as 90 parts per million [ppm] have been measured in cars carrying smokers. [A level of a mere 50 ppm in a factory is considered to be a danger calling for immediate action.]

Tobacco interests take issue with some of the statistics quoted here, but the evidence leaves no doubt that tobacco use is costly; questioning the significance of a few of these statistics merely amounts to quibbling over the price. One price estimate quoted by Dr. Ochsner put the cost of the work days lost from smoking-induced illness and disability at over three times the estimated profit from tobacco.

Effects of Smoking on Nonsmokers

Fire and Health Insurance

Even if you never touch a tobacco product, your health and your wealth are adversely affected by smoking. The higher death rates and hospitalization rates of tobacco users are reflected in your life insurance and health insurance costs and in your taxes, which could be lowered if it were not for the excessive Medicare and Medicaid costs incurred by smokers.

A large part of your homeowner's insurance premium covers fire hazards. Since half of all home fires are caused by smoking, your rates are much higher than they would be if nobody smoked. But the real tragedy is that 90 percent of cigarette-caused fires are the result of chemical treatment of cigarettes with "oxidizers" to keep them burning for up to half an hour even when they are not puffed on. Cigarettes that are not treated with incendiary additives will burn out in less than four minutes [as most European cigarettes do].[5] Many disasters could be prevented by a law requiring U.S. cigarettes to be as fire safe as those now made in Europe. Senators from tobacco states argue that we should not legislate to "protect people from their own carelessness," but fires kill and cripple innocent victims as well as the careless smokers responsible for starting them. We pay a heavy price for exempting cigarettes from all consumer safety regulations.

Second-hand Smoke

The deadly constituents of tobacco smoke find their way into the organs of nonsmokers as well as smokers. Some of these constituents include known cancer-producing agents such as radioactive lead (Pb-210), which is carried through the air to nearby nonsmokers.[6] The nonsmoker breathes more of the unfiltered smoke from the burning end of the cigarette, and this smoke contains a higher concentration of hazardous substances such as tar, ammonia, benzo[a]pyrene, and cadmium.

You might think that the pollution emitted from a tiny cigarette would be insignificant in comparison to the fumes from thousands of autos, trucks, and buses, plus factories and power plants. Does tobacco smoke really reach a high enough concentration to be a significant health hazard?

An article in *Science*[7] gives the figures, which should come as no surprise to persons who experience eye and throat irritation as well as headaches in a room full of tobacco smoke. Irritation comes from "respirable suspended particulates" (RSP), and these can be counted directly. It is known that the potent carcinogen benzo[a]pyrene is adsorbed by RSP, which lodge in the lungs. RSP levels in the absence of smoking (in homes, libraries, churches, and smoke-free restaurants) were found to range from 24 to 57 micrograms per cubic centimeter. The levels in autos with windows slightly open, traveling on major highways, were in the middle of this range. In contrast, in a church during a bingo game the level was 279 micrograms per cubic meter, or about nine times the level in that same church during services when the density of people was higher and thirty votive candles were burning. Other places containing smokers showed levels between 86 and 697, whereas the outdoor reading at those places averaged 46. The levels in the smoking sections of two restaurants were double the levels in the nonsmoking sections.

The measured figures were used to calculate that a nonsmoking officeworker who works forty hours per week in an office with a habitual smoker gets an RSP burden equivalent to smoking five cigarettes per day. And a nonsmoking nightclub entertainer who works forty hours a week and shares an apartment with a chain smoker is involuntarily smoking the equivalent of twenty-seven cigarettes a day. Although this smoking is done through the nose rather than the mouth, the effect is expected to be almost the same because most RSP are too small to be trapped by the nose before entering the lung.

There is now independent evidence that these poisons do have an effect on nonsmokers. An article in the *New England Journal of Medicine*[8] gave the results of a study of lung function in 2,100 men and women. It showed that "passive smokers" (nonsmokers exposed to above-average levels of second-hand smoke) "fell into the same state of impaired performance as the noninhalers and light smokers." This state was considerably worse than that of other nonsmokers who had not been so exposed.

It has also been shown that lung illness in young children whose parents smoke at home is twice as common as it is in children of nonsmokers. And in several studies of nonsmoking married women, those whose husbands smoked developed lung cancer at a higher rate than those whose husbands were nonsmokers. One of these studies, in Japan, involved 91,540 nonsmoking subjects whose husbands' smoking habits were studied. During a fourteen-year period, 174 of these women developed lung cancer. The difference in rate between the wives of smokers and those of nonsmokers was highly significant statistically. An American study involving 153 cases also showed a greater incidence of lung cancer for the smokers' wives, but the difference was not technically significant. There is a probability of 7 percent that it could have occurred via a random fluctuation (as described in chapter 3).[9]

These findings are incorporated in the 1982 *Surgeon General's Report on the Health Consequences of Smoking*,[10] which goes on to conclude that "for the purpose of preventive medicine, prudence dictates that nonsmokers avoid exposure to second-hand tobacco smoke to the extent possible."

Smoking During Pregnancy

One group of passive smokers cannot avoid exposure; these are the unborn babies of mothers who smoke during pregnancy. These babies' average weight at birth is six ounces less than that of babies whose mothers do not smoke, and the reduction in birth weight is greater for babies whose mothers smoked more. This "stunting of growth" comes from the action of nicotine and carbon monoxide on the circulatory system of the baby. The effect is more than a simple weight loss in some cases; infant mortality is increased by about 50 percent when the mother smokes during pregnancy.

Alcohol and Drugs

The most widely abused drug in the United States is alcohol. It is estimated that, of the 100 million or so adult consumers of alcohol in the United States, almost 10% are alcoholics. Alcohol abusers contribute

- 40% of all male admissions to state mental hospitals
- 40% of family-court caseloads
- 33% of all suicides
- 50% (or more) of all fatal traffic accidents
- 24% of deaths from all accidents

These figures come from the National Institute on Alcohol Abuse and Alcoholism.

The percentages don't tell the whole story. The total number of alcohol-related deaths in the United States per year is about 100,000. For comparison, there are about 20,000 homicides. Concern about crime sometimes becomes an obsession, but you are more likely to be killed by the drink in your hand than by a mugger on the street.

This applies to "social drinkers" as well as to alcoholics. Unfortunately, impairment of driving ability by alcohol is accompanied by unwarranted overconfidence in that ability. It is clear that persuasion does not work in these cases. We will reduce the death toll from alcohol only when we decide collectively that we want to do it and are willing to press for consistent enforcement of laws against driving while under the influence of alcohol. Do we want to?

Alcohol and Disease

Of the 100,000 annual deaths attributed to alcohol, about two-thirds are accidents, homicides, and suicides. The rest result from disorders such as cirrhosis of the liver (which claims 30,000 victims per year and is eight times as likely to occur if you are an alcoholic) and alcoholic psychosis (about 5,000 deaths per year). The bizarre effect of long-term alcohol use is displayed vividly in Korsakoff's syndrome, a type of selective amnesia that makes the victim totally unable to remember recent events, although memory of long past events is retained. Apparently damage occurs to the part of the brain that assimilates new information.

Although alcohol does not affect the environment as to-bacco smoke does, the resulting violent and erratic behavior has an effect on nonusers, to say the least. Another serious effect is that on unborn children; fetal alcohol syndrome is now considered the third most common cause of mental retardation at birth.

Other Drugs

The American teenager has no difficulty in obtaining a staggering (no pun intended) variety of drugs for "recreational" uses. Besides alcohol, there are amphetamines, hashish, marijuana, phencyclidine (PCP or "angel dust"), lysergic acid diethylamide (LSD), and even cocaine and heroin.

Marijuana is said by some to be the least dangerous of these, but that is not saying much. While it does not usually have the devastating effect of PCP or LSD, it is not a drug to be dismissed lightly. It is often asserted (without proof) that marijuana is less harmful than alcohol. Even if this were true, it would be meaningless because almost all users of marijuana also use alcohol, and the combined effect is worse than that of either one by itself.

It is difficult to give probabilities on marijuana and other "recreational drugs," because statistics are hard to collect and the number of long-term users is still relatively small. However, one study of 300 fatal highway accidents showed that 16% of the drivers had been using marijuana. That figure is surely significantly higher than the percentage of all drivers who are under the influence of this drug at any given time.

Although the statistics on human use are sketchy, effects of the psychoactive ingredient of hashish and marijuana—delta-9-tetra-hydrocannabinol, or THC—can be gauged from animal tests. Corrections must be made for animal size and for the fact that animal doses are often given orally. Blood tests have shown that the bloodstream absorbs 50% of smoked THC, but only 5% to 10% of THC ingested orally, so an oral dose of 5 milligrams of THC per kilogram of body weight is roughly equivalent to human consumption of three marijuana cigarettes containing 10 milligrams each. Such a dose is not abnormally high, as apologists for marijuana have claimed in criticizing these tests.

Rats and monkeys that have been given appropriate doses of THC have exhibited abnormal brain waves, impairment in learning motor skills, and unusually aggressive behavior. Tissues taken from the limbic area of the brains of these animals show structural abnormalities. These and other results of THC tests have been discussed by Dr. Gabriel G. Nahas.[11] The tests leave no doubt that THC does more than induce a state of euphoria and that, like alcohol, it can cause aggressive behavior with deadly consequences.

Unlike alcohol, marijuana does not produce a recognizable hangover. This is because THC is released very slowly from the brain, causing the hangover to be spread out over about a week. Heavy users may become chronically depressed and irritable without knowing the reason.

Chronic bronchitis and lung cancer are further hazards of marijuana. Precancerous lesions have been found in the lungs of twenty-one-year-old pot smokers. It has been estimated from such results that smoking only one marijuana cigarette is equivalent to smoking thirty-five regular cigarettes.

Marijuana has been advocated for treatment of glaucoma, but clinical trials cited by Dr. Nahas have shown that it is no more effective than pilocarpine hydrochloride, a drug that does not give the undesirable side effects of THC.

The untrained observer must be careful about drawing conclusions from casual observation of marijuana users. You must consider that the source of the product is totally unreliable. People who have said that it had no effect on them may have been smoking dandelion leaves, for all we know. On the other hand, users of marijuana have been seriously harmed by "joints" containing additives to give a bigger kick—things like PCP or strychnine are commonly used, according to doctors who have treated the victims.

However, as we have seen, marijuana by itself can have serious effects. Many psychiatrists diagnose victims as having "marijuana psychosis" characterized by paranoia bordering on schizophrenia. It is well established that marijuana is a serious danger to persons with a "tendency to schizophrenia." The trouble is that you might not know you have a "tendency to schizophrenia" until it is too late. In short, if you gamble on marijuana, the stakes are very high (unless you place no value on your brain).

The risk is particularly high for adolescents. Marijuana is known to inhibit cell division and as a result to retard the normal development of adolescents. Ironically, this is the group most likely to use marijuana.

More potent—and unpredictable—drugs such as PCP and LSD are said to be great fun for those who have "good trips." Unfortunately, you don't know when you'll have a "bad trip," and such trips can result in terrifying "flashbacks" that recur many months after the drug was used. So playing with these things is another version of Russian roulette, except that you have no idea of what the odds are—and neither do I. But if you watch, as I have done, when victims of this sport (some of them students of mine) are brought in to mental hospitals, you might conclude that the odds can never be right.

Cocaine is yet another drug that is considered by some to be relatively innocuous. It is the "in" drug among those who can afford it—sort of a status symbol in the bored-with-life crowd.[12] But it should be apparent from the many incidents involving celebrities that this drug can destroy you quite as effectively as other drugs. Just ask any cocaine user who is undergoing treatment to salvage his career.

Weapons

You have heard the slogans: "If guns were outlawed, only outlaws will have guns." "Guns don't kill people; people do." But slogans make a poor substitute for evidence. Let's look at the probabilities and the statistics.

First, the probability that all guns will be "outlawed" in the United States is zero. On the other hand, as Judge Marvin E. Aspen of Cook County pointed out, prohibiting the sale and possession of *handguns* would "create an absolute liability crime with which to charge the criminal who is caught in possession of a handgun; this alone is bound to aid law enforcement." The alternative, to enact automatic, severe penalties for committing a crime while carrying a gun, is of no use in catching a criminal or *preventing* crime. Three-fourths of all murders are impulsive acts, committed by people with no criminal record. For the rest, criminals are not noted for intellectual sophistication. Like children, they seldom worry about the consequences of their acts. To keep a child from playing with matches, would you threaten him or would you just keep the matches away from him?

As for the other slogan, people do use guns to kill people. Handguns are designed for killing, and they make some killings possible that could not have happened any other way. When a three-year-old kills a six-year-old, he doesn't do it with a hockey stick.

Although U.S. courts have ruled that the Constitution does not guarantee the right to have a handgun, it is still very difficult to enact laws controlling them in this country. Other countries have far more controls on them. As a result, in a typical year (1979), handguns killed: 48 people in Japan; 34 in Switzerland; 52 in Canada; 58 in Israel; 21 in Sweden; 42 in West Germany; 8 in England; and 10,728 in the United States.

People who oppose all types of gun controls are not worried by these numbers; they say it is "the price we pay for freedom." But the countries on that list can hardly be called dictatorships, and experience in past wars does not suggest that the so-called Saturday night special will be very effective in stopping a modern army.

Many gun owners are in favor of gun control. Perhaps they believe that, in the absence of effective controls on handguns, they had better have one, too, just for self-defense. However, according to Judge Aspen, "For every one intruder who is stopped with a gun, there are four accidental shootings, caused either by mishandling the weapon or by mistaking an innocent person for a criminal. There are 3,000 accidental deaths by firearms each year, and one-fourth of the victims are children under thirteen." It is natural to want to defend your property, but is it worth your child's life?

Motor Vehicles

Motor vehicle accidents cost about 50,000 lives and cause 1.7 million injuries each year in the United States. Half of those killed are occupants of automobiles. It is estimated that 12,000 of these lives could be saved and half of the injuries prevented if everyone wore seat belts at all times while in a moving vehicle. At present, fewer than one auto occupant in five wears a seat belt.

Some people will wear a seat belt on a long trip, but not for driving around town. The fatality rate in city traffic, however, is more than double the rate on freeways. The most preventable tragedies occur in collisions at 30 miles per hour or less. These accidents would produce only minor injuries if seat belts were worn.

In a head-on collision at 30 mph the front two feet of your car collapses, and the passenger compartment, relatively intact, comes to a stop in about one-tenth of a second. If you are not wearing a seat belt, your body continues forward at 30 mph until you hit something—the windshield, steering column, door post, etc. [see figures 14-1 and 14-2]. It is this second collision that causes the injuries and death. Unbelted, you are no more able to prevent the second collision than you can avoid hitting the ground if you fall off a cliff. Picture yourself running into a steel post at full speed—about 15 mph. How do you think 30 mph feels?

To bring your passenger compartment from 30 mph to a stop in 0.1 second requires an acceleration of about fourteen times the acceleration of gravity. If you are holding a 30-pound child in your lap, this 14-g acceleration makes the child "weigh" over 400 pounds. What is the probability that you can hold onto a load like that and keep the child safe? Almost zero, judging from accident records.

Some people say they would rather be "thrown clear" [through the windshield?] in an accident. If you think it is safer to be a human cannonball in highway traffic, you might have a great career in the circus. Analysis of many accidents shows that about one-fourth of all passenger and driver deaths result from being thrown out of the car. If you ride a motorcycle, you will always be "thrown clear" in an accident, and your probability of being killed, per mile, will be several times that of an automobile passenger.

Another objection to seat belts is that they might make it more difficult to escape if your car is on fire or submerged under water. But you can't escape if you are unconscious with a fractured skull. By preventing head injury, the seat belt keeps you conscious so you *can* escape. In a four-year period in Ontario [1972–1975], only three drivers wearing seat belts died in a car that burned or was under water. It is conceivable that one or two of them might have lived if they had not been wearing seat belts. On the other hand, during those four years, several thousand persons died in vehicle accidents in that same province, and at least a thousand could have been saved by seat belts. With odds of 1,000 to 1, why bet your life on the underdog?[13]

Numerous analyses of actual accidents have shown the number of lives that could be saved and injuries avoided if seat belts were worn. In one year [1974] in Canada, 2,529 drivers died in accidents. The death rate for unbelted drivers was about 2.38 per 1,000 accidents; the rate for belted drivers, only 0.85 per 1,000. A Swedish study of over 28,000 accidents showed that belted people receive about half as

Figure 14–1. Effect of a 30-mph head-on collision of an unbelted driver.

0.000 seconds—car hits barrier

On impact, the car begins to crush and to slow down. The person inside the car has nothing to slow him down so he continues to move forward inside the car at 30 mph.

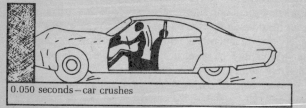

0.050 seconds—car crushes

The car slows down as the crushing of the front end absorbs some of the force of the collision. The person inside is still moving forward at 30 mph.

0.100 seconds—car stops
0.120 seconds—person hits car interior

One-fiftieth of a second after the car has stopped, the person slams into the dashboard and windshield. This is the human collision. In the car's collision it takes 1/10 of a second to stop; in the human collision it takes only 1/100 of a second.

SOURCE: *The Human Collision*, 2d ed. (Toronto, Ontario: Ministry of Transportation and Communications, 1976).

Figure 14–2. Effect of a 30-mph head-on collision when driver wears a seat belt.

On impact. the car begins to crush and to slow down.

As the car slows down. the person moves forward until the seat belts restrain him. The belts keep him in his seat and keep his head and chest from striking the car interior.

Being fastened to the framework of the car. belted occupants are able to "ride down" the collision as part of the car. They are able to take advantage of the car's slower stop. as it crushes and absorbs energy. For belted people there is no human collision.

SOURCE: *The Human Collision*, 2d ed. (Toronto, Ontario: Ministry of Transportation and Communications, 1976).

many injuries and suffer half as many fatalities as unbelted persons. [See figure 14-3.] This ratio holds at all speeds up to 60 mph.

In spite of these statistics, there is strong opposition to passage of laws requiring the use of seat belts. It is argued that laws would be ineffective in increasing seat-belt usage, but experience suggests otherwise. In Australia, the death rate from motor vehicle accidents was reduced by 27% after passage of a mandatory seat-belt law. It is likely that the reduction would be even greater if everyone obeyed the law, but the number of lives that are saved is what counts, and that number is impressive.

Prevention of injury and death has been achieved in the United States by passage of laws requiring the use of helmets by motorcyclists. When these [state] laws were first enacted in 1967, as a result of federal regulations, the death rate from motorcycle accidents decreased by about 50%. [The death rate is now about 4,000 per year.] But in 1976 Congress removed the penalties against states that did not meet the federal standards for helmet laws. In 1976 through 1979, twenty-seven states repealed or weakened their laws, and since then there has been a 40% increase in the death rate from motorcycle accidents in those states.[14]

One might question whether the government should try to protect people from the effects of their own bad decisions. But the taxpayers are expected to pay for treatment of injured people who cannot afford to pay, and the most effective treatment is prevention. Surveys have shown that about half of the hospitalized motorcyclists are not covered by insurance, and the taxpayers foot their bills. Many of these people become paraplegics who require care for the rest of their lives. If we are responsible for them at that point, why not assume some responsibility for them earlier when the results will be better?

Figure 14-3. Injuries and fatalities at various speeds, with and without seat belts.

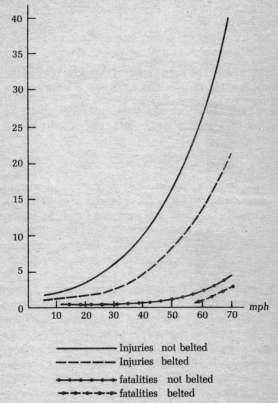

Percent killed or injured

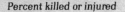

A Swedish study showed that belted people received about half as many injuries as unbelted people in collisions at all speeds.

SOURCE: *The Human Collision*, 2d ed. [Toronto, Ontario: Ministry of Transportation and Communications, 1976.]

Radiation

Radiation can be good or bad. The sun's radiation is eagerly sought, and the resulting tan is widely admired. But that same radiation also brings wrinkles and skin cancer. X-rays are a boon to surgery and dentistry, but they, too, cause cancer. Ionizing radiation from radioactive materials or nuclear reactors is greatly feared, but it can be very effective in diagnosing and treating cancer. It would also provide a great improvement in food preservation if it were given a chance.

Let's focus on the types of radiation that come from radioactive materials to see why these types are feared, whether that fear has a rational basis, and to what extent that fear may handicap us.

Radioactivity

When radioactivity was first discovered, it was thought that a radioactive substance was capable of emitting radiation "perpetually." It was then discovered that, in emitting radiation, an atom spontaneously changes [decays] into an atom of a different kind. Therefore the number of radioactive atoms, and hence the amount of radiation, decreases steadily with time.

When it decays, a radioactive atom normally emits alpha particles or beta particles. It may also emit gamma rays. An alpha particle is a nucleus of a helium atom. It cannot even penetrate a sheet of paper; it poses little danger when its source is outside your body. However, it is highly dangerous to swallow or inhale a source of alpha particles, because they will deposit all of their energy within a very short distance, often in a sensitive organ of your body.

Beta particles are electrons, either negatively or positively charged. They, too, are not very penetrating; they can be stopped by a thin sheet of metal [about a millimeter], so here again the principal danger comes when the source gets inside your body.

Gamma rays are high-energy electromagnetic radiation [like X-rays]. Some of them can penetrate an inch of lead, so they can be hazardous even when the source is tucked away in a concrete block.

The number of atoms that decay in a given period of time is governed by the laws of probability. If the species in question has a ''half-life'' of, say, one hour, then for each atom there is a probability of 1/2 that it will decay within an hour.[15]

If we start with one trillion radioactive atoms that have a half-life of one hour, an hour later there will be *about* half a trillion of them left. [The precise number will vary in accordance with the ''normal distribution''; see chapter 3.] After another hour we will have one-quarter trillion of the original atoms, and three-quarters of a trillion ''daughter'' atoms, which may or may not be radioactive themselves. After about forty hours, only one of the original trillion atoms will remain. That survivor will have a 50% chance of surviving still another hour, just as it had a 50% chance of surviving each of the first forty hours.

It is said that plutonium-239 [Pu-239] is very dangerous because of its long half-life [24,000 years]. But uranium-238 [U-238], which occurs naturally, has a half-life of billions of years. Nuclear reactors, which convert U-238 atoms into Pu-239 atoms, must therefore be making the world safer for future generations, right?

That doesn't seem right. We must have overlooked something. Let's take another example, one that is on a more human time scale. Compare Pu-239 with lead-210 [Pb-210], which has a half-life of 22.3 years. Our friend Morris is unlucky enough to inhale a particle containing a trillion [10^{12}] atoms of Pu-239 [about 400 picograms, or 4×10^{-10} grams]. His brother Boris inhales a trillion atoms of Pb-210. Which one is in more danger from radioactivity?

In both cases, the material is too heavy to be easily eliminated by the body. In the 22.3-year half-life of Pb-210, half a trillion of Boris's Pb-210 atoms will have decayed, sending alpha particles into his lung. Morris will get a much smaller number of alphas, because the Pu-239 half-life is so much longer.

In general, if a species has a very long half-life, the fraction that decays in one year is equal to about 0.7 divided by the half-life in years, so about 0.003 % [0.7/24,000] of Morris's Pu atoms will decay each year. That makes the total number of alpha particles he absorbs in 22.3 years equal to 650 million instead of 500 billion—quite a difference. So, on this time scale, the material with the *shorter* half-life is more dangerous, for a given number of atoms. Similarly, if we worry about our descendants over the next few millenia, Pu-239 is more dangerous, per atom, than U-238.

Radiation Dose

How much damage does such a huge number of alpha particles actually do? To answer that question, radiologists consider a quantity called the radiation dose, which is the amount of energy deposited per gram of tissue. The unit of dose is called the "rad," technically defined as 100 ergs per gram. If all of the energy from those half-trillion alpha particles were deposited in one gram of Boris's lung tissue, the dose to that gram would be about 40,000 rads. If such a dose were received all at once by each gram in his whole body, Boris would die immediately.[16]

The biological effects of radiation are not related in a simple way to the dose received because the energy absorbed can do different things, from total destruction of a cell to temporary impairment of one of the cell's functions. The effect depends on the type of radiation, among other things. Observation of victims has shown that a given dose of alpha particles has roughly the same effect as a beta or gamma ray dose that is ten times as large. For this reason, a unit called a "rem" has been defined in such a way that each rad of beta or gamma radiation is about one rem, but each rad of alpha radiation is roughly ten rem.

A dose of over 600 rems to the whole body is almost always fatal if it is delivered over a period of a few days because it destroys the bone marrow. [However, persons receiving such doses have survived when an arm or a leg was shielded, permitting the bone marrow there to provide new blood cells.] Doses of between 400 and 600 rems can cause death; the probability increases with the dose, being about 50% at 500 rems. Doses of 100 to 400 rems cause nausea, fatigue, hemorrhaging, and lowered resistance to infection, but the victim usually recovers if cared for. Doses of 25 to 100 rems cause changes in blood cell counts, but the recipient usually feels little effect.

Smaller doses cause no immediately observable effects, but they damage cells, resulting in decreased life expectancy. A whole-body dose of 100 rems has been observed to cause some form of cancer in about 2% of those who received it. [This number has been determined by comparing an exposed population with an unexposed control population.] It has also been found that, in the range of 100 to 200 rems, the "excess" cancer rate in the exposed population is directly proportional to the dose. It is impossible to gather sufficient statistics to demonstrate what the effect is at doses much below 100 rems; the conservative assumption is that the probability of getting cancer is directly proportional to the dose all the way down to zero dose. In other words, one rem gives cancer to 1 person in 5,000, one-tenth rem gives cancer to 1 person in 50,000, and there is no "threshold" below which radiation is perfectly safe.

How does this relate to the dose that you are likely to receive in everyday life? This dose comes from a combination of natural radiation from radioactive materials in the environment, cosmic radiation from outer space, medical and dental X-rays, and even radioactive matter inside your body. Potassium-40, an unavoidable constituent of living matter, is a beta emitter with a half-life of about one billion years. Your body also contains hydrogen-3 [tritium] and carbon-14, which are produced in the atmosphere by cosmic rays.

The average dose to a person living at sea level in the United States from all these sources combined is about one-sixth of a rem per year, or enough to cause cancer in 1 out of 30,000 persons [about 8,000 cases per year in the entire United States]. About half of this dose comes from manmade sources, primarily diagnostic X-rays. The remainder is divided about equally among cosmic radiation, terrestrial radiation from the environment, and radioactive materials within the body.[17]

Leakage from nuclear power plants contributes an average dose of about 0.003 rem per year—enough to cause 100 to 200 deaths annually in the United States. [I will not speculate on the odds against a catastrophic increase in that leakage. Calculations of these odds are based on so many assumptions that they mean very little. But it does seem ironic that many nuclear power protesters can be seen deliberately inhaling smoke that contains radioactive lead.]

Some of your radiation exposure is subject to your control. You can be careful not to permit diagnostic X-rays unless they are essential. In 1974, Sidney M. Wolfe, M.D., of the Public Citizen Health Research Group, estimated from published data[18] that more than half of the diagnostic X-ray dose received at that time by residents of the United States was unnecessary. If your doctor or dentist resents being questioned about proposed X-ray doses, considering it a challenge to his "professional competence," his competence may well be in question. A truly competent practitioner will not be afraid of questions. You have a right to know what the odds are when you bet your life.

Your exposure also depends on where you live, because cosmic rays are more intense at higher altitudes, and stone houses contain more radioactive material than wooden ones. Cosmic ray intensity doubles with each mile increase in altitude. Thus citizens of the "mile-high city" get an additional dose of about 0.03 rem per year, or enough to increase the probability of cancer by about one in a million every two months. The same increase results from living in a stone building for two months. [For comparison, this is equal to the risk from smoking a total of two cigarettes.] Building materials all contain traces of radium, which is not a problem in itself; but one of the "daughters" of radium is radon, a radioactive gas that escapes from the material and that is dangerous when inhaled. The magnitude of this problem is not completely determined at present, but it is known that sealing a home very tightly [to conserve energy] can raise the radon concentration by a factor of ten!

Your occupation obviously can affect your radiation dose.

An airline pilot who flies at an altitude of about seven miles receives cosmic radiation at a rate of about 128 (2^7) times the sea-level rate. This gives him (and each of his passengers) an additional chance in a million of getting cancer for each ten hours of flying time. But this is considerably smaller than the probability of dying in an airline crash during that amount of flying time, which itself is a very small probability (less than 1 in 100,000).

One reason why radioactivity is so feared is that it can cause genetic changes. A single hit by a gamma ray on a gene can alter it, causing a "mutation" that is usually not desirable. This effect is well documented in insects, such as the ever-popular fruit fly, which reproduces so rapidly that many generations can be studied during the period of one research grant. It is clear that radiation-induced mutations can also occur in human beings, but we have no statistics on this. You can't make guinea pigs (or fruit flies) out of human beings.

Induced Radioactivity

Some people have the misconception that anything exposed to radiation is likely to become radioactive itself, and hence it is dangerous. It is true that some kinds of radiation can induce radioactivity; this is what happens in a nuclear bomb or a nuclear reactor. But irradiation with X-rays or gamma rays of moderate energy (the energy of gamma rays emitted by most radioactive atoms) does not affect the atomic nucleus, so it cannot cause the transmutation that makes a stable atom radioactive. The damage caused by this sort of radiation comes solely from its action in breaking chemical bonds that hold together the molecules in our bodies.

For this reason there should be no fear of the process of preserving foods by irradiation, a process that has been known for decades to be effective and economical. Irradiation, which would kill viruses and insect eggs, would surely be preferable to the current practice of using pesticides, some of which are suspected carcinogens. Unfortunately, we are often afraid of the wrong things. It seems that pesticides,

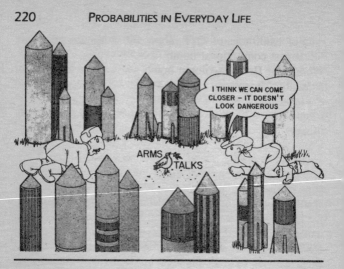

Nancy A. Burgard

food preservatives, and additives cannot be banned until we prove beyond the shadow of a doubt that they are dangerous, but irradiation cannot be permitted until we prove beyond any doubt that it is totally innocuous. This illustrates the rule that unfamiliar things are frightening, even when we don't worry about more familiar things that can be many times as dangerous.

Nuclear Weapons

The unprecedented destructive power of nuclear weapons has led to speculation about the probability that a nuclear "exchange"[19] will occur. It is difficult to assign a probability to an event that has never occurred. However, wars have occurred, nuclear weapons of all sizes have been exploded, and volcanoes have erupted violently. Experience from such events tells us what actions may increase or decrease the probabilities of various outcomes.

To assess these probabilities, we need to understand the power of the weapons. This power is measured in "kilotons." One kiloton equals the energy released by the explosion of 1,000 tons of TNT, about 500 times the energy of the largest conventional bomb [the "blockbuster"] used in World War II. A 14-kiloton bomb was used at Hiroshima. Present nuclear weapons range in energy from about 1 kiloton to 10 megatons [10,000 kilotons]. One megaton in electrical energy would power 1 million all-electric homes for a month.

Tactical Weapons

"Small" bombs in the range of 1 to 10 kilotons are designed for battlefield use and are called "tactical" weapons. But as you see from the above figures, the destructive power of such a weapon is not small by any standard that we are accustomed to. For example, let us consider the controversial "neutron bomb." It has a yield of about 1 kiloton, and it was sold as a weapon that could kill enemy tank personnel without destroying property. It is intended to explode at an altitude of half a mile over enemy tanks, producing enough radiation, in the form of neutrons,[20] to deliver a dose of about 8,000 rads to "ground zero"—directly below the blast. [Each rad from these neutrons is equivalent in biological effect to about 7 rads from gamma rays.] This will ensure that even a person who is shielded by his tank will receive thousands of rems. [Such a large dose is necessary to ensure that the victim is killed promptly; a smaller lethal dose might permit him to function for hours or days, accomplishing whatever objectives he had been given.]

The ability of the neutron bomb to kill so promptly by radiation has led to many misconceptions about the weapon. This bomb certainly does destroy property; it creates an "overpressure" of about 2 pounds per square inch [psi] beneath it, which creates 70 mph winds. Concrete structures can withstand it, but wooden structures and windows are destroyed. [An overpressure of only ½ psi will break windows.] Furthermore, it cannot be aimed like a "death ray"; the neutrons fly out in all directions, killing friend, foe, and farmer. The approximate dose to an unshielded person at various distances is:

Distance from ground zero:	0.5 mile	1 mile	1.25 miles
Dose [rads; 1 rad = 7 rems]:	1,600	100	25
Chance of survival:	zero	zero	90%

In addition to 10% prompt fatalities at 1.25 miles, there will be an additional toll of about 10% from delayed effects [cancer].

In spite of the large area over which people would be killed or injured, a single neutron bomb is expected to knock out no more than five or six tanks, because of the spacing of the tanks, the fact that the tank crews are shielded by the tank itself, and the necessity to kill them quickly to stop the tank. So only the tanks within a few hundred yards of ground zero will be stopped, and halting a full-scale attack would require several hundred neutron bombs.

Aside from neutron bombs, several "civilized" countries have arsenals of tactical nuclear weapons. At this writing, the United States has about 20,000 and the Soviet Union about 12,000, and both are adding to their supplies daily. Most of these weapons would be detonated close to ground level for maximum blast effect in the immediate area. This would also produce maximum fallout, as the dust blown up by the explosion spreads radioactive debris over a wide area.

Tactical weapons are said to be necessary to make our deterrent "credible," it being considered incredible that we would use our larger weapons in a situation where the United States itself was not under direct attack. But General Omar Bradley pointed out in 1949 that proposals to use tactical nuclear weapons were "folly," because if "millions of invader troops moved into Western Europe," how could we "use the bomb against them without killing ten friends for every foe?" Is this how we show our European allies our "commitment" to them?

It is not necessary to have access to military plans in order to assess the *relative* probabilities in this situation. Every additional "tactical" nuclear weapon that is deployed increases the probability that a full-scale nuclear war will develop. This statement is based on the following pure logic: [1] To make these weapons "credible," authority to use them is given to more people.[21] [2] People make mistakes, and people sometimes act irrationally. [3] The use of one nuclear weapon reduces the inhibition against using others. Q.E.D.

Former Defense Secretary Robert McNamara said that the resulting "risk of bungling into a confrontation that nobody wants, that nobody planned, that nobody intended, is very high." Some people are willing to run this risk of full-scale nuclear war because of a belief that the possibility of such a war is the only thing that has maintained peace between the Soviet Union and the United States. This is an unprovable assertion. When the Soviet Union had no nuclear weapons, the United States did not attack Eastern Europe to "liberate" it, simply because such a move would be a gamble with a highly negative expectation. Is it only the fact that we have nuclear weapons that kept the Soviets from attacking Western Europe? Couldn't it be that the Soviet leaders recognize that their own expectation on such a gamble would also be negative, with or without the threat of *nuclear* retaliation? Even if their conventional weapons slightly outnumber ours, it is well known that attack requires considerably more strength than defense. According to the Center for Defense Information, NATO actually leads the Warsaw Pact in military spending, military manpower in uniform, and total ground forces in Europe.[22]

The irony of the present situation is that the major conflict of interest between the two superpowers is in the weapons themselves. If a war begins, the most likely cause will be the fear by one side of the other side's weapons. That is certainly what brought us close to war in 1962. So much for the weapons' peacekeeping ability.

On the other hand, the threat to escalate a war by using any kind of nuclear weapon has consequences that dwarf anything that we can imagine. Let us try to imagine the unimaginable by looking at the properties of strategic nuclear weapons.

Strategic Weapons

The term "strategic" has come to describe a weapon that is carried by an intercontinental ballistic missile [ICBM]. These weapons can come in all sizes. The MIRV carries as many as ten bombs, or warheads, on one missile ["vehicle"].[23] Each bomb may have an energy (yield) of about 40 kilotons, and each can be directed to a different target when it nears its destination. Other strategic weapons can carry one megaton or more in one bomb.

The area of destruction produced by a ground-level explosion is proportional to the two-thirds power of the yield, so a one-megaton bomb, which releases seventy times the energy of the Hiroshima bomb, would produce comparable devastation over an area seventeen times as great, or at a distance about four times as far from ground zero. But 400 kilotons in the form of ten 40-kiloton bombs would do even "better"; each would take care of an area twice as great as that destroyed by the Hiroshima bomb, making the total area of devastation twenty times as great as at Hiroshima. So the MIRV, carrying ten bombs at once, has led to the development of smaller weapons with more destructive capacity.

For any given yield, the destruction produced at any distance from ground zero is well known. Table 14-2 gives the facts for a one-megaton bomb; you can work out the results for any other yield from the fact that the distance is proportional to the cube root of the yield. The numbers give just a small part of the picture; for more details of the destruction, see "Effects of Nuclear Weapons" by Leo Sartori.[24]

Deterrence

The superpowers now have enough nuclear weapons to cause this sort of devastation for thousands of targets. If a sizable fraction—say 10%—of them were fired, the result would most probably be prompt death for most of the superpowers' population and lingering death for the rest of the people in the world. It has been calculated that explosion of a total of 500 to 1,000 megatons would trigger a "nuclear winter;" clouds of dust would blanket the earth, cutting off sunlight for so long that food would disappear and human beings would become extinct (in much the same way that dinosaur extinctions are believed to have been triggered by the impact of an asteroid on earth 65 million years ago).

Even if a nuclear winter did not set in, it is 100% probable

Table 14-2. Effects of Nuclear Weapons

Distance from point of explosion	Effect of one-megaton bomb	
	Heat and light	*Blast*[a]
2 miles	100 calories per cm² [200 times the sun's brightness, for 20 seconds]	20 psi; 500 mph wind; concrete structures destroyed
4 miles	25 cal/cm²; ignition of clothing	5 psi; 160 mph wind; brick and wood houses demolished; chance of survival zero
7 miles	10 cal/cm²; third-degree burns; blindness if one looks at blast	2 psi; 70 mph wind; damage to roofs, walls, and windows

a. Distances for pressure effects are proportional to cube root of yield and therefore would be one-tenth as great for one kiloton.

SOURCE: Leo Sartori, ''Effects of Nuclear Weapons,'' *Physics Today*, 36 [March 1983], table 2, 37. Copyright 1983 by the American Institute of Physics. Adapted by permission.

that the death toll would not end when the explosions were over. Many burn victims would die a slow, painful death with no treatment, no pain killers. Radiation poisoning would reduce resistance to disease, which would spread rapidly in an environment polluted by decaying bodies. Whatever his faults, Nikita Khrushchev spoke the truth when he said, ''The survivors will envy the dead.''

Leaders of both superpowers assure us that they know these facts and that their policy decisions are intended to prevent the disaster that threatens us. Each side must keep its weapons to avoid ''nuclear blackmail'' by the other—that is, as a deterrent to keep the other side from using, or threatening to use, nuclear weapons. But the word *deterrent* has been used very loosely.

It is one thing to keep nuclear weapons to deter nuclear

attack. But to think that you can deter anything else with them leads to a moral issue that cannot be avoided even if you believe that some wars are justifiable. Moralists considering this issue have concluded that there is never a moral justification for using nuclear weapons to fight a war.

The issue is whether, when a man attacks you, you are justified in killing his family and everybody else in his neighborhood in retaliation. Some might say this could be justified if it prevented future attacks and thus led to a net saving in human life; these are the grounds for justifying the use of nuclear weapons in World War II. But using nuclear weapons on an attacker *who is also armed with such weapons* is certain to increase the loss of life on both sides and quite probable to end the existence of both nations. Under these conditions, the threat of using these weapons is as clever a ''deterrent'' as wearing dynamite around your belt to repel would-be attackers on the street.

Yet leaders persist in talking of this kind of deterrence and of trying to make it credible by invoking new kinds of weapons (both offensive and defensive) that will ''limit'' the damage to one's own side. Some leaders have disavowed their previous assertions that nuclear war is winnable, but they still proclaim preposterous objectives: ''If deterrence fails, we will prevail.'' Marvelous—not ''win,'' but ''prevail.'' To prevail seems to mean that, at any point during the mutual annihilation process, our side will always have more weapons left than their side. What good that will do us is never made clear. Here is a brief look at the prospects.

First-strike Weapons

First-strike weapons are designed to eliminate an enemy's missiles before they are fired. They are presumably so accurate that they can make a direct hit on an enemy missile silo—that is, a hit close enough to produce the 1,000 psi or so necessary to destroy a hardened underground silo. With MIRVs it is not hard to build enough of these to wipe out all the enemy's missiles, because one MIRV, with ten warheads, can knock out ten missiles in their silos.

Unfortunately, the same advantage accrues to your enemy,

provided that he strikes first. If your enemy has missiles that can wipe out your weapons, and you can wipe out his first, there is an enormous temptation to strike first. There is also great tension because of the fear that your enemy will strike first to grab this perceived advantage.

The only way to counter this advantage is to "launch on warning"—to launch your missiles during the brief time after you detect that theirs have been launched, but before theirs arrive. Of course in such a situation it would be pointless to attack the enemy's now-empty silos, so you hit their cities, and in a short time, it is all over.

So while it is superficially attractive to make more accurate missiles so you can destroy those of the enemy, in reality it is a futile, destabilizing maneuver that increases the probability of war by accident or fear.[25] Another monumentally futile endeavor is to build defensive systems, although that also is attractive to politicians who don't understand the realities of these weapons.

Defensive Systems

Albert Einstein said, "The unleashed power of the atom has changed everything save our modes of thinking." Nowhere is this more true than in the search for a defense against nuclear weapons. If people attack you with arrows, you can use a shield; one shield stops many arrows. Cannonballs fired at ships can be stopped by armor plate. But to stop a nuclear missile requires more than a shield; it requires either another missile (an ABM) or a technology that hasn't been invented yet ("Star Wars" defense in space).

People say, "If we could send a man to the moon, why couldn't we invent such technology?" Maybe we could, to stop a certain number of missiles. But we would need a system that is 100% effective against any number of missiles. If 100 missiles are launched toward Chicago, and you stop 98% of them, Chicago no longer exists. The Soviets built an ABM system around Moscow capable of stopping 32 missiles. When they deployed it, we responded by targeting more missiles on Moscow.[26]

The point is that missiles are far cheaper to build than to

defend against, and nothing that is remotely imaginable will change that. Furthermore, when we sent a man to the moon, there was no enemy trying to stop us. A laser system in space could be put out of action by a well-aimed BB gun. Would we be prepared to begin a nuclear war if the Soviets sabotaged our lasers before they were operational?[27]

All of these "defensive strategies," relying on marvelous technological "fixes" that exist only in artists' drawings, are nothing more than daydreams. Do we dare indulge in such fantasies in place of hard negotiations? Instead of planning what to do if deterrence fails (which is a way of increasing the probability that deterrence *will* fail), we need to make sure that it will *not* fail. This is not done by more weapons; we had enough of those years ago. Anybody who thinks that we need a greater variety of nuclear weapons to be flexible has no conception of what the things do.

What we really need is a president who will negotiate with the sole objective of reducing the nuclear danger and not confuse that objective by trying to emerge with a better strategic position. That's just a formula for stalemate and continued danger. It is difficult to negotiate with a determined enemy, but it is impossible to survive any other way.

Perspectives

Table 14-3 summarizes some gambles of this chapter by listing activities that carry a risk that we regularly accept—a probability of one in a million that death will result from the activity. (I omit nuclear warfare because the absolute probabilities are unknown.) The purpose of this comparison is not to scare you, but rather to put things into perspective, so you can direct your energies toward avoiding the really big hazards.

It makes no sense to shrug your shoulders and do nothing about the big hazards on the rationalization that "everything is hazardous." It isn't. Earth is a hospitable planet; if it were not, human life would not have survived as long as it has. But for one reason or another, mankind has created a wide variety of hazards. We can minimize these, for ourselves and

Table 14-3. Activities with a One-in-a-Million Risk of Death

Activity	Duration or amount
Driving (auto)	Sixty miles, no seat belt; 120 miles with seat belt
Motorcycling	Two miles, no helmet; 5 miles with helmet
Flying (commercial jet)	Ten hours (because of cosmic radiation); one takeoff and landing (risk of accident)
Flying (private plane)	Four minutes (risk of accident)
Living in Denver	Two months (because of cosmic radiation)
Living in a stone house	Two months (because of radon from radium in walls)
Smoking	Two cigarettes or $\frac{1}{20}$ of a ''joint''

for our descendants, if we know what they are and are willing to exert ourselves. By finishing this book, you have shown that you are willing to exert yourself.

NOTES

Chapter 1: Principles and Propositions

1. Sometimes we must be careful about our assumptions. If the coin belongs to somebody else, the coin's owner may know a good reason for the coin to come up heads rather than tails. According to Gina Kolata ["Prestidigitator of Digits," *Science 85*, April 1985, 66-72], statistician-magician Persi Diaconis can toss a coin and make it come up heads every time.
2. We always refer to a "large" number of trials to avoid the problem of statistical fluctuations in the results. We shall see how to tackle that problem in chapter 2.
3. We can say this, but it might not always be true. A more clever person might find a reason that we missed. See note 1.
4. Oswald Jacoby, *How to Figure the Odds* [Garden City, N.Y.: Doubleday, 1947], 119-20.
5. Despite what astrologers may say, this is an excellent assumption, even if all the people are neurosurgeons whose hobby is skydiving. See chapter 3 for a discussion of statistics in astrology.

Chapter 2: Statistics

1. Quoted in Eliot Mashall, "EPA's High-Risk Carcinogen Policy," *Science* 218 [1982], 975.

Chapter 3: Uses and Abuses of Statistics

1. The rem is a unit of radiation dose. The "average" person in the United States gets about ⅙ rem per year from all sources. See chapter 14.
2. Reported by E. Kral, "The Teacher, the Student, and Reports of the Paranormal," *The Skeptical Inquirer* 7, no. 4 [1979], 42.
3. According to the publisher's introduction to a book by [who else?] Linda Goodman, *Linda Goodman's Sun Signs* [New York: Bantam Books, 1968].
4. While not all people listed in a directory of scientists are exclusively scientists, they have achieved something in the field to set them apart from nonscientists, so the test is unambiguous.

5. *Linda Goodman's Sun Signs*; R. C. Davison, *Astrology* [New York: Arco, 1963], 148, in which Davison says, "The sun may show the native's occupation by its sign . . ."; Evangeline Adams, in *Astrology for Everyone* [New York: Dodd, Mead, 1931], 14, says, "All Aries people tend to succeed in public life."

6. For example, M. E. Crummere, in *Sun-Sign Revelations* [New York: Viking, 1974], 27, says that "the seriously intellectual Gemini is capable of becoming an important scientific researcher . . ." For a summary of such claims, see "PSI Astronomy Unit: Astrology—The Space-Age Science?" M. Zeilik II, *American Journal of Physics* 42 [1974], 538-542.

7. Quoted by T. Hines, "Biorhythm Theory: A Critical Review," *The Skeptical Inquirer* 3, no. 4 [1979], 26.

8. Tests are described in Hines, "Biorhythm Theory," 26.

9. Ibid.

10. Ibid.

11. Arnold L. Lieber, *The Lunar Effect* [New York: Dell, 1978], 26-27.

12. This is not the place for a detailed discussion of "tides," except to say that they cannot possibly be connected with water retention in a body on land [Lieber's mechanism for the effect] and that the effect varies inversely with the cube of the distance from the attracting body. Thus, a car parked in your driveway has a far bigger tidal effect than the moon as far as your body is concerned. You can work this out for yourself with the aid of any elementary physics book, or you can consult your friendly neighborhood physics professor for verification. [A believer in the tidal effect could say that this discussion explains why some people go crazy at parties. It's because of all those cars parked in the driveway!]

Chapter 5: The House Percentage

1. H. Steinhaus, *Mathematical Snapshots*, 3d ed. [New York: Oxford University Press, 1969], 35.

2. From an interview on national television, quoted in Edward O. Thorp, *Beat the Dealer* [New York: Random House, 1966], 74. In this book Thorp presents his blackjack system, which is described in chapter 6. Blackjack is the only casino game in which the player can have the edge if he works hard enough.

3. Reported by Warren Weaver in *Lady Luck* [Garden City, N.Y.: Anchor Books, 1963], 156-61.

4. Edwin Silberstang, *Playboy's Guide to Casino Gambling*, vol. 4: *Baccarat* [Wideview Books, 1980], 71.

Chapter 6: Blackjack

1. Thorp's system appears in his book *Beat the Dealer* (New York: Random House, 1966), chapter 5. In recent years other systems, also based on computer-tested strategies, have been published. It is unlikely that any of these systems differ enough from Thorp's to justify the price of the books, let alone the extra effort involved in learning them. As long as you have a system that works (and Thorp's clearly does), your biggest problem is to use it without being thrown out of the casino. Ian Andersen gives interesting advice on this in *Turning the Tables on Las Vegas* (New York: Vanguard Press, 1976), 37-50.

2. One popular book on gambling says that it is a clever bet to insure if you have a natural yourself. It is true that insuring on a natural guarantees you a net profit equal to your original bet. But it throws away a chance for a bigger profit; it reduces your overall expectation. Why back halfway out of a bet that you are a favorite to win? You went to the casino to gamble, didn't you?

3. For advice on how to do this, see Andersen, *Turning the Tables on Las Vegas*.

Chapter 7: Horse Racing

1. This can happen, theoretically, even in a place pool or a win pool, but I have never seen it.

2. It would be just as convenient to round down to multiples of $.10. The track pays an odd multiple of $.10 when it saves them money; they pay $2.10, not $2.20, on a minus pool.

3. You'll have to decide which horse you like. I can't help you there.

4. Obviously you can't rely on these figures if you bet too soon. The numbers can change quickly because many other bettors can also spot a bargain. You may be shut out if you wait until the last minute, but you'll be better off in the long run. If you don't bet, you can't lose.

5. Your profit comes from the money bet on the losing horses. When favorites finish out of the money, there is more profit to share.

6. A famous scam involved driving up the odds on a heavy favorite by making last-minute bets on all the other horses in the race. Meanwhile, other members of the betting syndicate placed bets with bookmakers on the favorite and collected at the inflated track odds.

Chapter 8: Sporting Chances

1. Earnshaw Cook, *Percentage Baseball* (Cambridge, Mass.: M.I.T. Press, 1966), 7.

2. Two other small possibilities do not change this conclusion. If both runners are safe, the scoring chance goes up to 60%. If the bunt is turned into a double play, the scoring chance sinks to 7%.

3. Bill James, *The Bill James Baseball Abstract* [New York: Ballantine Books, 1983], 96.
4. Statistics for 1982 were found in the *Bill James Baseball Abstract*. Further statistics were kindly provided by the Atlanta, Cincinnati, Houston, Philadelphia, St. Louis, and San Diego baseball clubs.
5. Some call it the "permit" defense.
6. If the chance of success were 10% or more, the "bomb" would be thrown more often, and over 100 points would be scored in each game.
7. We also ignore the possibility that the quarterback will be sacked—thrown for a loss—because this has to be small, for an experienced quarterback in this field position, with the option of throwing the ball beyond everybody.

Chapter 9: Contract Bridge

1. Any card smaller than the tenspot is referred to as "x."
2. East's ten cards outside of spades and low diamonds include two clubs that he has already played, but these club plays tell you nothing about how many clubs he was dealt (except that he was dealt at least two, which was overwhelmingly probable anyway). Therefore, the number of clubs he has played does not affect the odds (just as the number of spades that you see in Proposition 1 does not affect the odds).

Chapter 10: Poker

1. Oswald Jacoby, *Oswald Jacoby on Poker* [Garden City, N.Y.: Doubleday, 1947], 1.
2. One poker-playing computer has been described by N. V. Findler, "Computer Poker," *Scientific American*, 239, no. 1 [July 1978], 144-51. It was said to have done very well against experienced human players.
3. If each of the four opponents holds a pair and then each draws three cards, the chance that none of them will improve is $(.71)^4$, which works out to about 26%.
4. Six possible pairs of aces and six possible pairs of kings can be dealt from a full deck to one of your opponents. If you hold an ace and a king yourself, the number of pairs of aces that an opponent can hold is reduced to three, as is the number of pairs of kings. So a total of six pairs can beat your queens, just as a total of six pairs can beat a pair of kings when all four aces are available. And the fact that you can keep the ace as a kicker makes your hand even stronger than an aceless hand with a pair of kings.

Chapter 11: Other Friendly Games

1. John R. Crawford, *How to Be a Consistent Winner in the Most Popular Card Games* (Garden City, N.Y.: Doubleday, 1961), ch. 3.
2. Contrast this with the odds in bridge, where game is a winning proposition even if the odds are slightly against making it. If you are not making five out of six hands when you freely bid 400, you are bidding too much.
3. We neglect the small chance that you will lose on both your first and second turns by rolling a 2-1 each time.
4. Oswald Jacoby and John R. Crawford, *The Backgammon Book* (New York: Bantam Books, 1973).

Chapter 12: Insurance

1. Some policies pay the cash value plus the face value in the event of death, and therefore the actual protection remains constant. But you pay for what you get; premiums are higher on such policies.
2. The overall mortality rate for women of that age is about 2 per 1,000, or 30 per 15,000, so the company's "house percentage" is well over 40%, considering that Prudence is a "preferred risk."
3. See chapter 14.
4. The most likely explanation for the higher nonwhite mortality rate is economic. Although in the United States the total number of poor white people exceeds the total number of poor nonwhites, a higher percentage of nonwhites are poor. Poor people can't afford good medical care nor can they afford to buy life insurance.
5. These numbers are derived from the Poisson distribution discussed in chapter 2. We saw there that, if m is the average, or mean, number of events, then the chance that zero events (losses) occur is e^{-m}, the chance of one loss is $m e^{-m}$, and the chance of n losses is $(m^n/n!)e^{-m}$ (where e is the base of natural logarithms, about 2.71828182845904 . . .).
6. This is a reasonable assumption given what we see the same companies charging for the accidental death benefit on life insurance.

Chapter 13: Investments

1. Five toy Salvation Army soldiers were sold in London in 1979 for £280. Their original price in 1930 was twopence each. That means the price increased by a factor of 6,700, for an annual growth rate of about 20%. Of course if somebody had saved a carload of those toys and tried to sell them in 1979, it would have been a different story. It is always easier to make a big percentage gain when you start from a small base.

Chapter 14: You Bet Your Life

1. Reported by S. Lichtenstein et al., "Judged Frequency of Lethal Events," *Journal of Experimental Psychology: Human Learning and Memory* 4 (1978), 551-578.

2. From P. Slovic et al., "Facts and Fears: Understanding Perceived Risk," in *Societal Risk Assessment: How Safe is Safe Enough?* edited by R. Schwing and W. A. Albers, Jr. (New York: Plenum Press 1980), 181-214.

3. T. Hirayama, "Epidemiological Aspects of Lung Cancer in the Orient," in *Lung Cancer 1982*, edited by S. Ishikawa, Y. Hayata, and K. Suemasu (Amsterdam: Excerpta Medica, 1982), 1-13.

4. P. V. Cole, "Comparative Effects of Atmospheric Pollution and Cigarette Smoking on Carboxyhaemoglobin Levels in Man," *Nature* 255: 699.

5. See Donald D. Trunkey, "Trauma," *Scientific American* (August 1983), 28-35. Dr. Trunkey points out that most furniture, upholstery, and mattresses made in the United States need more than four minutes' exposure to a burning cigarette for ignition.

6. According to E. A. Martell, "Tobacco Radioactivity and Cancer in Smokers," *American Scientist* 63 (1975), 404, Pb-210 particles get into tobacco from soil treated with phosphates from uranium-rich rocks. Lead-210 has a half-life of twenty-two years; once in your lungs, it stays there, like plutonium, irradiating the delicate tissues.

7. James L. Repace and Alfred H. Lowrey, "Indoor Air Pollution, Tobacco Smoke and Public Health," *Science* 208 (1980), 464.

8. J. R. White and H. F. Froeb, "Small-Airways Dysfunction in Nonsmokers Chronically Exposed to Tobacco Smoke," *New England Journal of Medicine* 302 (27 March 1980), 720-23.

9. The Japanese results are reported by T. Hirayama, *British Medical Journal* 282 (1981), 183-85, and discussed in the same journal on pages 914-17 of the next volume, 283. The Tobacco Institute claimed in a press release that "several U.S. experts had found an apparent statistical error in the Japanese calculations." In fact, it had merely been speculated that an error might have occurred; experts who carefully checked the figures found that this error did not occur. Another objection was that pipe smokers, who also are "passive" smokers of their own smoke, show no increased incidence of lung cancer. This is simply false.

10. *U.S. Surgeon General's Report on the Health Consequences of Smoking* (Washington, D.C.: U. S. Government Printing Office, 1982).

11. Gabriel G. Nahas, "Current Status of Marijuana Research," *Journal of the American Medical Association* 242 (1979), 2775-78.

12. Some say that the widespread use of cocaine in Hollywood is responsible for the unfunny comedy shows that have proliferated on TV.

13. Data are from *The Human Collision*, 2d ed. (Toronto: Ministry of Transportation and Communications, 1976). The Swedish study was

reported by N. I. Bohlin in *Eleventh Stapp Car Crash Conference Proceedings* [New York: Society of Automotive Engineers, 1967].

14. Donald D. Trunkey, "Trauma," *Scientific American*, August 1983.

15. It could decay at any time during that hour. The probability that it will decay in the first minute is about 1.15%, and the same probability holds for each succeeding minute. Combining all these probabilities gives the 50% probability for decaying within an hour.

16. Of course, the total energy Boris received would then be much higher because his body mass is many thousands of grams.

17. Much of this information is given in Arthur C. Upton, "The Biological Effects of Low-Level Ionizing Radiation," *Scientific American*, February 1982, 41-49.

18. Department of Health, "Report of State and Local Radiological Health Problems, Fiscal Year 1972," Education and Welfare publications [FDA] 73-8047, and "Population Exposure to X-rays, U.S., 1970," [FDA] 74-8004. Dr. Wolfe's estimate appears in Priscilla Laws, "Medical and Dental X-rays" [Washington, D.C.: Public Citizen Health Research Group, 1974].

19. "Exchange" is a euphemism for simultaneous destruction of "targets" [e.g., the state of Kansas] in opposing countries.

20. Neutrons reside in atomic nuclei and are released in nuclear reactions that occur in bombs or reactors. Being electrically neutral, they have a penetrating power like that of gamma rays. The presence of two "extra" neutrons is what distinguishes radioactive Pb-210 from the nonradioactive lead isotope Pb-208.

21. One nuclear-weapons analyst, Paul Bracken, said that once a war started, there would be "such chaos and confusion that decentralized decision-making would become a de facto reality." "A Defect in the Limited War Theory," *Science*, 223 [1984], 1271. No military leader has been found to disagree with that assessment.

22. *The Defense Monitor* 13, no. 6 [1984], 5.

23. MIRV is an acronym for Multiple Independently Targetable Reentry Vehicles.

24. *Physics Today* [March 1983], 32-41.

25. Dare I accuse our "experts" of superficial thinking? Consider this. As reported by Elizabeth Drew ["A Political Journal," *New Yorker*, 20 June 1983, 55], one expert, James Woolsey, said in 1981, "To deploy MX in existing silos, hardened or not, provides little more than a fig leaf, and that, at best, for only a short time." Sounds pretty strong. But in 1983, the same Woolsey was chief author of the Scowcroft Commission report that recommended placement of the same MX in the same existing silos! His flipflop was not unusual. Although the original rationale for the missile was proclaimed in this report to be erroneous, a new one was invented; and when thirty-five basing modes for the missile were found to be unsuitable, one of them was resurrected anyway. According to Ms. Drew, "The MX drove the rationale,

rather than the other way around—the rationale kept changing.'' That sort of expertise does not inspire confidence.

26. Most leaders of the work on defensive systems agree that cities cannot be protected. Their objective is to build a system that threatens to shoot down enough enemy missiles to save some of our own missile silos from a first strike. They argue that even a system that was not sure to work would deter a first strike, because an enemy could not be sure of destroying our ability to strike back. [But that situation already exists, because our submarines are invulnerable and will continue to be for the foreseeable future.] However, Robert Jastrow, in *How to Make Nuclear Weapons Obsolete* [Boston, Mass.: Little, Brown, 1985], goes further. He claims [page 113] that a four-stage defense ''can be made nearly perfect.'' He says that 99.8% of attacking warheads could be stopped if each stage stopped 80%. The arithmetic is correct; if a given missile has a 20% chance of penetrating each stage, its chance of reaching its target is $.2^4$, which is .0016 or about 0.2%. Unfortunately, the 80% figure is a pure guess. If you assume that 50% are stopped by each stage, then 6% of the warheads escape, and the ''shield'' becomes a sieve. Even 50% is a wildly optimistic figure for destruction of warheads in space after decoys have been released. Jastrow's book is reviewed by R. L. Garwin in *Physics Today*, 38, no. 12 [1985], 75-78, and discussed further in *Physics Today*, 39, no. 3 [1986], 9-15, 142-48.

27. Noted physicist W. K. M. Panofsky, in ''The Strategic Defense Initiative: Perception vs. Reality,'' *Physics Today*, 38, no. 6 [1985], 34-45, said, ''Space-based weapons are more vulnerable than ballistic missiles in any part of their orbits.'' He continued, ''I know of no responsible study . . . that indicates that the competition between the marginal cost of ballistic missile defense and that of offensive countermeasures even remotely favors the defense.''

INDEX

239

ABOUT THE AUTHOR

John D. McGervey is a professor of physics at Case Western Reserve University. He earned his B.S. from the University of Pittsburgh and an M.S. and Ph.D. from the Carnegie Institute of Technology (now Carnegie-Mellon University). He is author of *Introduction to Modern Physics* and numerous articles on physics, teaching physics, general science, and contract bridge (he became a Life Master in bridge at the age of twenty-two). He has participated in many community activities including Educators for Social Responsibility and is listed in *Who's Who in America*.